THE TUNIC BIBLE

One Pattern, Interchangeable Pieces, Ready-to-Wear Results!

C&T PUBLISHING

Publisher: Amy Marson

Creative Director: Gailen Runge

Editors: Lynn Koolish and Joanna Burgarino

Technical Editors: Debbie Rodgers and Helen Frost

Cover/Book Designer: April Mostek

Production Coordinator: Tim Manibusan

Production Editor: Jennifer Warren

Illustrator: Lon Eric Craven

Photo Assistant: Carly Jean Marin

Style photography by Chris Smith unless otherwise noted

Published by C&T Publishing, Inc., P.O. Box 1456, Lafayette, CA 94549

Library of Congress Cataloging-in-Publication Data

Names: Gunn, Sarah, 1956- | Starr, Julie, 1957-

Title: The tunic bible : one pattern, interchangeable pieces, ready-to-wear results! / Sarah Gunn and Julie Starr.

Description: Lafayette, CA : C&T Publishing, Inc., [2016]

Identifiers: LCCN 2016014302 | ISBN 9781617453564 (soft cover)

Subjects: LCSH: Tunics. | Sewing.

Classification: LCC TT546 .G86 2016 | DDC 646.2--dc23

LC record available at https://lccn.loc.gov/2016014302

Printed in China

10 9 8 7 6 5 4 3 2

Dedication

From Julie

For Jim, whose love, support, and belief that I can do anything I put my mind to means the world to me

For my mom, who teaches by example always and in all things

From Sarah

In memory of my father, Don Welch, for showing me how to live creatively and think outside the box

Acknowledgments

We are incredibly grateful to the many talented people who helped make our book a reality!

- To the fine staff at C&T Publishing for enthusiastically accepting our proposal and investing in two new authors—we especially thank editors Roxane Cerda, Lynn Koolish, Joanna Burgarino, and Debbie Rodgers; designer April Mostek; and production team Tim Manibusan and Jennifer Warren.

- To Chris Smith of Chris and Cami Photography for his extraordinary talent and commitment to *The Tunic Bible* (while overcoming floods, dusk, and deadlines!)

- To Robbin Knight of Robbin Knight Photography, LLC, for the generous use of his Charleston studio space

- To *The Tunic Bible* contributors, for expanding the vision of our pattern with fresh ideas and inspirational sewing— these incredible sewists bring unmeasurable energy, talent, and imagination to the garment sewing community.

   We would specifically like to thank Sallie Barbee, Sonja Gingerich, Marcy Harriell, Tracey Hogan, Beth Huntington, Manju Nittala, Deepika Prakash, Dorcas Ross, Bianca Springer, Lucy VanDoorn, Lori VanMaanen, Andrea Verbanic, and Cissie Wellons.

- To Jennifer DeShazer of Jennuine Design, whose patience and technical talents brought our pattern to life

- To our cute models: Caroline Cotter, Brittany McDougal, Grace Caroline Price, Mary Catherine Price, Branea Reeves, Crystal Rogers, and Margaret Todd Truluck

- To the Vendue Inn, a premier Charleston hotel, for providing access to its stunning property for many photographs

- To our friends and neighbors in and around Charleston and Kiawah Island, South Carolina, for graciously providing the settings for many of our photos

- To Mood Fabrics for generously supplying a vast array of textiles to the blog, *Goodbye Valentino*, thus providing a unique opportunity to develop sewing skills and fabric expertise

- To the *Pattern Review* website and the online sewing community for making us better sewists

- To Kathie Bennett, a dear friend and publicist extraordinaire

- To Sarah's mother, Nancy Welch, for making her learn how to sew and helping her along the way

- To Sarah's cute husband, Billy Gunn, whose support is always present through skillfully snapping photographs, providing heartfelt opinions of her new creations, and promoting her sewing endeavors to everyone he knows

- Finally, to the *Goodbye Valentino* blog readers—there would be no book without you.

CONTENTS

INTRODUCTION

Considered one of the earliest known garments, the tunic continues to rank as a global wardrobe mainstay due to its stylish versatility and flattering silhouette. From simple and modest to daring and chic, women sport fashionable tunics from the beach to the ballroom—any setting, any scene, any season!

Wikipedia defines a tunic as "any of several types of garment for the body, usually simple in style, reaching from the shoulders to a length somewhere between the hips and the ankles. The name derives from the Latin *tunica*, the basic garment worn by both men and women in Ancient Rome, which in turn was based on earlier Greek garments."

We like a definition that inspires the imagination—and we hope *The Tunic Bible* will inspire you! Your tunics can be as simple or as elaborate as you choose. Whether your aesthetic is everyday casual, preppy chic, bohemian, or glamorous, creating the ideal tunic for your style is now easily achievable with only one book.

Our top priority as sewists is to bring high-end and mainstream ready-to-wear fashion to our beloved hobby. While duplicating a favorite ready-to-wear piece produces quite a thrill, sewing a garment *inspired* by our favorite designers honors our originality. On the practical side, we love the ability to fit, sew on demand, and make a fashionable garment for a fraction of the cost of buying it ready to wear!

We are proud to belong to a group of home sewists that exceeds 35 million creative women and men in the United States alone. Through the website *Pattern Review* (sewing.patternreview.com), which currently has more than 300,000 members, the two of us quickly discovered that we shared similar sewing backgrounds, taste in apparel, and an enormous desire to learn more. Best of all, we both live in South Carolina!

As two women who love wearing tunics, we began focusing on the details that characterize our favorite tunic brands, such as Devon Baer, Eileen Fisher, Elizabeth McKay, Gretchen Scott, Jude Connally, Lilly Pulitzer, Sail to Sable, Sheridan French, and Tory Burch. We realized the tunic bodice remains consistent. Changing a single detail, such as the neckline, placket, trim, or collar, often affects a tunic's entire appearance. This led us to our *aha* moment: one bodice, interchangeable components, and endless possibilities!

The Tunic Bible, a one-stop pattern and look book, combines all of the components needed to construct an unlimited number of fashionable tunics. Written for home sewists, the book is ideal for all ranges of sewing skills, from basic to advanced. It includes a tunic pattern featuring one bodice that is adaptable to multiple styles, lengths, necklines, collars, and sleeve-finishing options. Interchangeable pattern pieces provide opportunities to produce multiple tunic styles without purchasing multiple patterns. In addition to the tunic pattern, *The Tunic Bible* provides assembly instructions for each optional component, an overview of bodice fitting, directions for embellishing with trims, fabric and supply resources, inspiration photos, and tips on creating tunics with professional, ready-to-wear results.

We recognize and value the manner in which technology has extraordinarily supplemented physical sewing get-togethers through blogging, virtual classes, online pattern reviews, and social media. Since we know sewing with friends creates magical synergy, we have launched a *companion* website, thetunicbible.com, to keep the creative juices flowing.

So now it's time to sharpen your scissors and put the pedal to the metal. Let's sew!

—*Sarah Gunn and Julie Starr*

HOW TO USE THIS BOOK

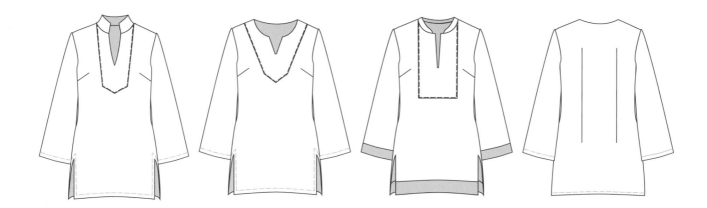

You've come a long way, baby!

To follow the evolution of the tunic is to follow the development of mankind, for the two are inseparable. Born in ancient Egypt as a simple rectangle with a center hole, the tunic became the primary garment for millions of people living in those early civilizations.

Roman tunics featured bands of different widths, colors, and ornamentation, which identified class and status. In the Middle Ages, tunics were elaborately embellished with gold threads and braids. The simplicity of the tunic proved a perfect platform for showcasing developing textile skills, leading the garment to fulfill numerous fashion, religious, and military purposes. Understandably, the tunic has maintained its appeal for men and women for thousands of years, because it is functional, comfortable, and fashionable.

To get the most benefit from *The Tunic Bible*, we suggest you use the book in the following order:

- Identify your style by exploring the elements of the tunic (page 10). Notice how fabric choices affect the tunic's silhouette and the way trims transform the appearance of the garment. Discover how neckline and sleeve combinations work together by perusing Tunic Formulas: Mixing and Matching Tunic Elements (page 48).

- Find inspiration by looking at the featured gallery of tunics (page 32) by thirteen talented bloggers and online sewists. Their personalized interpretations of the main tunic pattern demonstrate its possibilities in ways we could not have imagined.

- Make a bodice out of muslin using the instructions in Fitting Your Muslin (page 45).

- Review Resources (page 108) as necessary, should your bodice need adjustments. We have listed our favorite online alteration tutorials, classes, and books for additional help.

- Once fitted, it's time to bring your muslin to life by choosing your fabric, neckline, sleeves, length, and trims.

- Check the information in Supplies, Notions, and Accessories (page 43) to be sure you have the right tools for the job.

- Locate the specific elements you have chosen in the sewing tutorials section (page 66).

Tip

Remember, making a muslin to test placket and neckline finishes always ensures success. Even ready-to-wear clothes designers make multiple muslin versions before cutting into expensive fashion fabric.

- Finally, use General Assembly Order (page 47) to find the proper tunic construction order.

NECKLINES AND COLLAR COMBINATIONS

Whether decorative or functional, the neckline frames the face and distinguishes the overall style of a garment. Inspired by our favorite ready-to-wear tunics, the following neckline options provide a multitude of possibilities to ignite your sewing mojo!

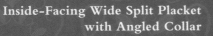

**Inside-Facing Wide Split Placket
with Angled Collar** **A**

B **Outside-Facing Wide Split Placket
with Angled Collar**

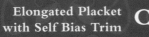

**Elongated Placket
with Self Bias Trim** **C**

D **Elongated Placket
with Band Collar**

Photo by William Gunn

A. Inside-Facing Wide Split Placket with Angled Collar

This placket and collar combination is perfect for a chic and polished look! The wide split placket opens the neckline, creating a dramatic angle for our signature collar. The collar width easily accommodates your choice of trim. When turned to the inside, the placket provides a crisp outline for decorative trim.

B. Outside-Facing Wide Split Placket with Angled Collar

When the placket is turned to the outside in contrasting fabric, it needs no further embellishments and makes a statement on its own.

C. Elongated Placket with Self Bias Trim

One piece of contrasting fabric is all it takes to complete this look! The companion bias trim brings balance and flair to the narrow, elongated placket. No additional trims or ribbons are required! The elongated placket and bias trim work well with a bias neckline finish.

D. Elongated Placket with Band Collar

Or try the elongated placket with no bias trim and a simple band collar.

E. Inside-Facing V-neck Placket

F. Outside-Facing V-neck Placket

Easy to sew and easy to embellish, this neckline is always a winner! A perfect choice for your first tunic, this collarless option is the most versatile of all the necklines in this book. The V-neck shape is well suited for nearly any fabric. The beauty of this neckline is its simplicity. Turn it inside for a clean finish or outside for a contrasting look!

E Inside-Facing V-neck Placket

F Outside-Facing V-neck Placket

Ruffle Neckline: Small Ruffle **A**

B Ruffle Neckline: Full Frill

C Scoop Neckline

A. Ruffle Neckline: Small Ruffle

B. Ruffle Neckline: Full Frill

Franz Liszt famously said, "Truth is a great flirt," and so are a few ruffles! Transform your tunic into the quintessential feminine garment. Add a small ruffle just around the collar or go for the full frill around the neck.

C. Scoop Neckline

Designed just for knits and finished with a knit binding, this technique easily produces results with a ready-to-wear quality.

Shorty Placket **D**

E Shorty Placket

Bib Placket **F**

D. & E. Shorty Placket

Would you believe these tunics feature the *same* placket? The Shorty, a wide-width placket, might be the most versatile of all! It nicely accommodates neckline appliqués, and the larger surface area is a great platform for embroidery, which is very effective when used on a simple contrasting placket.

F. Bib Placket

We designed this playful finish for lightweight fabrics and casual garments, but notice Tracey Hogan's sophisticated take in our gallery photos.

SLEEVES

Let your sleeves do the talking!

Trimmed, tailored, or whimsical, the sleeve makes a powerful statement about your garment. A simple change in sleeve style can transform the personality of your tunic. Our sleeve options leave the decision up to you!

Split Cuff **A**

B Ruffle Cuff

Sleeve Cuff **C**

A. Split Cuff

The split cuff lends an air of refinement to any tunic. Choose a traditional-length cuff in a contrasting fabric for a sporty look, or create some drama with a big, bold cuff!

B. Ruffle Cuff

Keep it feminine with a unique ruffle sleeve finish. Whether placed above or below the elbow, this fun option never fails to be noticed!

C. Sleeve Cuff

This cuff provides an effective finish to your sleeve. We suggest a 2˝ (5.1 cm) cuff and often sew this feature in contrasting fabric. Interfaced for stability and shape, this crisp sleeve detail will showcase your favorite bangle or bracelet.

Photo by William Gunn

Split Sleeve

A subtle alteration results in a major design change! Splitting the sleeve pattern creates a trendy vibe to any tunic.

Trimmed Sleeve

Finish the basic bell-shaped sleeve with decorative trims and ribbons—a perfect alternative to the cuff.

Sleeveless Armscye Finish

Hot hazy days call for cool sleeveless tunics! The cut-in shoulder elongates the arm and is finished with self-made (or purchased) bias tape.

BODICE SILHOUETTES

Tailor your tunic to best highlight your unique shape!

Some prefer a loose fit while others prefer fitted;

wouldn't you love to try both?

FIT — The starting point for our bodice pattern is the classic relaxed fit. We include back darts for customized shaping and suggest a side zipper for those who desire an even closer fit.

Loose Fit

Linen and lightweight fabrics are great choices for those seeking stylish comfort. This unstructured silhouette is ideal for casual living.

Tailored Fit

A *fitted* tunic? But of course! Many of our favorite ready-to-wear tunics are shaped from the back. Easily turn your tunic into a fitted beauty with two contoured back darts. Heavier fabrics and longer lengths often require more structure for a flattering fit. An invisible side zipper (page 107) is recommended for fitted tunics sewn in nonstretch fabrics.

Photos by William Gunn

LENGTH

Tunic lengths are as varied as the women who wear them! Our pattern includes three lengths as starting points to guide you toward the most flattering hemline for your tunic.

A. Tunic Length

This length is a great choice to pair with leggings, skinny jeans, shorts, and capris. It should end just above or below the widest area of your body.

B. Dress Length

This all-occasion style opens up a world of one-piece dressing possibilities. Dress and go!

C. Maxi Length

The reinvented maxi is a ubiquitous fixture on the fashion scene. Paired with flip-flops, the ankle-grazing length brings a fresh approach to street-style dressing. Or take it out on the town in silky fabrics and heels. A summer staple, the maxi is always a great option for looking hot while staying cool. Try one!

LOWER-EDGE EMBELLISHMENTS

Side Slits

Side slits not only allow freedom of movement but also brilliantly showcase decorative trims.

Trims

Embellish your tunic from top to bottom. Repeating the trim along the hem completes your look with a cohesive punctuation mark!

Contrasting Hem Band

What a great complement to the contrasting placket! Our contrasting hem band tutorial (page 100) demonstrates a 3˝ (7.6 cm) band that is well suited for all lengths. For those looking for an alternative size, customizing the width of this band takes no time at all.

Border Prints

Strategically placed border prints function as striking embellishments for any tunic length!

Photo by William Gunn

OUR FAVORITE FABRICS

Linen

Embrace those wrinkles! Natural linen looks best when it's beautifully rumpled. Linen tunics exist in every color combination imaginable, from tone-on-tone to stark contrasts, and inspire us to sew, sew, sew! Lightweight linens are perfect for a classic loose fit, while midweight linens are suitable for fitted dress-length tunics.

Linen fabrics will nicely showcase embellishments, including heavy braids, ribbon, twill tape, beaded appliqués, and contrasting plackets.

Tip

Linen qualities greatly vary. The top weaving mills are in Italy, where the process to create the finest linen in the world has been handed down through generations. Ultra-soft linen is most desirable, but don't despair if your linen appears a little stiff. Regarded as the world's strongest natural fiber, linen becomes softer with every wash. Prewashing linen at least once is a must.

Cotton

Versatile, breathable, low-maintenance, and affordable, cotton is a perennial favorite for tunic construction. While *cotton voile* catches the breeze on hot summer days, *cotton broadcloth* withstands the wear and tear of the daily grind. *Cotton flannels* bring fall festivities to life and are also a great choice for tunic nightshirts and pajamas. Easy to embellish, cottons rarely pucker when ribbons and trims are applied.

We urge cotton purists to consider the newer stretch cottons that are blended with Lycra. Many ready-to-wear labels feature this friendly fabric throughout their collections due to its ability to maintain a flattering shape. We also highly recommend cotton voiles blended with silk for their beautiful drape, light weight, and strength.

Tips

· Always prewash cotton material before sewing.

· For the front and back bodice, use two layers of lightweight voile to eliminate transparency. Leave the sleeves sheer for a chic touch.

Photo by William Gunn

SILK

Whether your goal is to dress up your jeans or to sew for a gala, look no further than silk! Once considered an extravagance and reserved for royalty, silk is now widely available in a variety of designs and price ranges. Don't be scared of silk—while it looks and feels delicate, many silks are strong and sew without complications.

A. Silk Twill

Our number one favorite type of silk is the finely woven *silk twill*. A sturdy fabric with a lovely drape, it is ideal for the classic loose fit. The texture of silk twill makes this fabric user friendly provided it is handled with care. Most ready-to-wear labels rarely embellish silk with trims, preferring simple details to let the beauty of the silk shine on its own.

B. Silk Dupioni

Silk dupioni isn't just for bridesmaids! The infinite choice of vivid colors of dupioni is too tempting to forgo. Dupioni, unlike other silks, maintains a rough texture and is compatible with dramatic embellishments.

While dupioni is easy to sew, the fabric requires special attention to achieve a professional finish. Underline dupioni with a soft cotton to attain a pliable fabric quality. (See Resources, page 108.)

The featured dupioni tunic is underlined in cotton. Consider dupioni or *silk taffeta* for a fitted tunic dress with a dramatic ruffled neckline.

Other Silks

Other silks such as *crepe de chine* and *charmeuse* produce beautiful tunics. We prefer the traditional loose fit and short length for these fabrics. These delicate and expensive fabrics, however, are trickier to sew. We do not recommend them for beginners.

Tips

· Clean your silk fabric before sewing.

· Once the pieces are cut, all markings such as darts and stitching lines should be thread traced.

· Baste all your seams to keep the fabric from slipping under the presser foot, which results in a distorted seamline. Silk can slip even with a walking foot.

· Learn more about sewing with silk in Resources (page 108).

· Remember, simplicity is the key to sewing a successful silk tunic!

A Silk Twill

B Silk Dupioni

KNITS

Knits, knits, knits—easily the most versatile fabric in your wardrobe! Easy to dress up or down with a change of accessories, a knit tunic becomes a truly welcome travel companion.

Today, nearly every fiber is available in a knit form! We like to identify knits according to the following categories: stable knits, midweight knits, and lightweight knits. All are tunic worthy!

Tip

Depending upon the amount of stretch in your fabric, you may find it necessary to size down when using knits.

Stable Knits

Beefy stable knits, such as *double knits* and *ponte*, produce attractive tunic dresses. *French terry* and *sweatshirt fleece* are unexpected and cozy choices for cooler-weather tunics.

This black Tory Burch sweatshirt fleece tunic inspired us to try our own version in green French terry.

While fabric choices generally dictate the style and fit of a garment, stable knits work equally well loose or fitted. These fabrics may be considered too heavy for applied contrasting plackets but work well with twill tape and petersham ribbon embellishments.

Color blocking is another great option for adding an unexpected detail to the heavier knit tunics.

A. Midweight Knits

Consider midweight knits, such as *silk jersey, viscose,* and *cotton jersey,* for maxi dresses. Their ability to nip and flare in all the right places produces a flattering fit not achievable in other weights. Best of all, these fabrics are suitcase friendly!

B. Lightweight Knits

Lightweight fabrics such as *linen knits* and *bamboo jersey* should be simple and loose for an easy chic look. Try the scoop neckline with knit binding (page 84) designed just for knits or the inside-facing V-neck placket (page 78) for a smooth neckline option.

Tips

· When sewing with knits, always staystitch the neckline and armscye immediately upon cutting to prevent distortion. (See Resources, page 108.)

· Apply a 1˝ (2.5 cm) piece of fusible knit interfacing around the lower edge of heavy- and midweight knits to stabilize the hem.

· Consider sewing a matching tank top to wear under transparent knits.

A Midweight Knits

B Lightweight Knits

OUR FAVORITE FABRICS

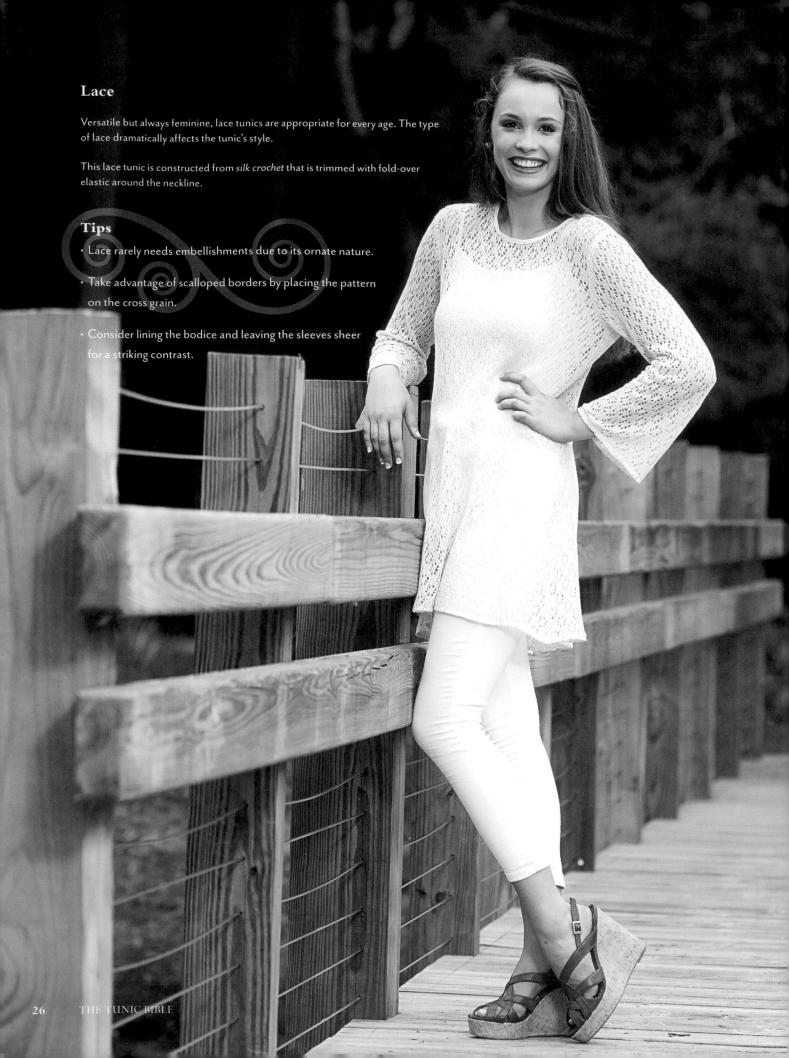

Lace

Versatile but always feminine, lace tunics are appropriate for every age. The type of lace dramatically affects the tunic's style.

This lace tunic is constructed from *silk crochet* that is trimmed with fold-over elastic around the neckline.

Tips

· Lace rarely needs embellishments due to its ornate nature.

· Take advantage of scalloped borders by placing the pattern on the cross grain.

· Consider lining the bodice and leaving the sleeves sheer for a striking contrast.

WHITE FABRICS

We believe white fabrics deserve their own category!

Each spring, the ready-to-wear tunic labels introduce a new collection of fresh white tunics; this inspires us to do the same, but in our own way, of course! Whether sewn in sheer voile, eyelet lace, silk, or linen, the white tunic yields pristine, chic results.

White fabrics are the perfect canvas for customizing your style. We think the secret to success when sewing in white is to mix textures. Once you start creating white tunics, you'll never stop!

The combination of linen and voile balances the light and heavy weights (bottom right). Textured ribbon, combined with smooth cotton, produces a subtle textural contrast (above). In the dotted voile tunic (below), the fabric design is echoed with pom-pom trim.

Tips

• Keep your hands clean!

• Trace the pattern markings with white tracing paper and then thread trace them in a contrasting color. (See Resources, page 108.)

• The tonal variation of off-white combined with pure white is especially sophisticated!

Photo by William Gunn

Photo by William Gunn

Think Outside the Bolt

Once a tablecloth, not always a tablecloth! Who can resist the urge to repurpose? Scarves and pashminas are a favorite repurposing choice, with vintage sheets being a close second.

The tunics above were constructed from a Gretchen Scott scarf (right) and an Indian sarong by Roberta Roller Rabbit (left).

Tips

· Don't forget to visit the scarf display in stores for economical fabric finds *and* finished edges!

· Vintage sheets are often finished with hand-crocheted edging—perfect for sleeves and hems.

TRIMMING THE TUNIC

Consider tunic embellishments as frosting on the cake. Ribbons and trim add richness and variety, which yield the sought-after ready-to-wear look. Simple trims bring extraordinary beauty through added dimension. Our favorite trims include twill tape, woven ribbon, open cording, beaded appliqués, and novelty offerings. Tunic plackets are the ideal spot to showcase embroidered custom design, while monograms look fabulous in a tucked-away spot.

Please note that all trims should be laundered or steam pressed before application to prevent shrinkage.

Twill Tape

Twill tape is readily available in a multitude of colors. It is a matte-finished, flat-woven ribbon usually made of cotton or polyester (and occasionally of linen) in varying widths and thicknesses. Twill tape can't be beat for flexibility and ease when mitering corners around plackets and side-seam slits. Due to its looser weave, twill tape is extremely forgiving and easy to shape around those tricky turns. A sporty row or two of twill tape against a contrasting solid-color fabric is always effective. Try combining different widths for a striking visual impact. You can find this trim decorating the edges of Sail to Sable tunics, one of our favorite ready-to-wear lines.

Petersham Ribbon **A**

B Woven Jacquard Trims

C Beaded Trim and Appliqués

A. Petersham Ribbon

Rayon or cotton petersham is the clear winner in the ribbon department. Its pliable picot scalloped edge allows it to be easily steamed around neckline curves. Petersham's lovely sheen also makes an especially striking counterpoint to linen. Do not confuse petersham with polyester grosgrain ribbon, which has a sealed or bonded edge. Both petersham and grosgrain are ribbed, but that is where the similarities end. Petersham is sold in many widths and shades.

B. Woven Jacquard Trims

Jacquard trims feature intricately woven embroidered designs and lend textural elegance to your tunic, which imparts a luxurious feel. Offered in a vast array of patterns, trims loomed on jacquard weaving machines produce a product that has complex definition. Jacquard trims can be composed of cotton, silk, metallic fibers, wool, acetate, and rayon. Scout estate sales and flea markets for exquisite vintage and novelty trims and ribbons. Swiss- and French-made jacquards are of the finest quality. These trims are best for straight runs because they accommodate folded angles well. They are also a Tory Burch favorite.

C. Beaded Trim and Appliqués

Bring on the bling! Beads, crystals, pearls, and sequins will transform your tunic into ornate evening and special-occasion wear. Premade jeweled appliqués may be applied to plackets with hand stitching or clear permanent fabric glue. Think Bollywood!

Rickrack **D**

E Mini Pom-Poms

Self-Made Bias Trim **F**

D. & E. Rickrack and Mini Pom-Poms

These playful trims, once thought to be reserved exclusively for children's wear, are fun to work with and add a whimsical vibe to beach cover-ups, casual summer tunics, and sleepwear.

F. Self-Made Bias Trim

We love using self-made bias trim. The Clover Press Perfect Hot Hemmer is the secret to making sharp-edged bias tape quickly with precise results. (See Supplies, Notions, and Accessories, page 43.) Size the trim however you like and then use it wherever you want!

GALLERY

Unleash your creative potential and make the tunic your own! These popular online sewists bring new energy and even more possibilities to tunic making with their original interpretations.

**Tracey Hogan,
featherstitchavenue.com**

Bib placket (page 86). Fitted sleeve. Modified ruffle cuff (page 91). **TUNIC FABRIC:** Embroidered cotton eyelet (two pieces). **TRIM:** Pintuck and embroidered cotton. **LENGTH:** Dress.

Photo by Santiago Vanegas

Photo by Tim Wallace

A. Cissie Wellons,
sewing.patternreview.com/members/CissieW

Outside-facing wide split placket (page 70).
Angled collar (page 72). Contrasting split cuffs (page 89).
Hem bands (page 100) with side slits (page 99).
TUNIC FABRIC: Embroidered silk organza.
TRIM: Silk dupioni. **LENGTH:** Tunic.

B. Deepika Prakash,
founder of sewing.patternreview.com

Ruffle neckline (page 82). Sleeveless armscye finish (page 97).
TUNIC FABRIC: Wax print cotton. **TRIM:** Piping. **LENGTH:** Tunic.

C. Bianca Springer,
thanksimadethem.blogspot.com

Shorty placket (page 85). Ruffle cuff (page 91).
TUNIC FABRIC: Dutch wax fabric. **LENGTH:** Dress,
hemmed to mini.

A

B

C

Photo by Deepika Prakash

Photo by Lisa Baldin

Dorcas Ross,
patternreview.com/members/ArtAttack

Ruffle neckline (page 82). Sleeveless armscye finish (page 97).
TUNIC FABRIC: Cotton. **LENGTH:** Dress.

Photo by Dorcas Ross

Photo by Martin Mogaard

Photo by Lori VanMaanen

Lucy VanDoorn,
myloveaffairwithsewing.com

Contrasting outside-facing wide split placket (page 70). Split cuffs (page 89). Angled collar (page 72). Side slits (page 99). **TUNIC FABRIC:** Cotton voile panel. **LENGTH:** Tunic.

Lori VanMaanen,
girlsinthegarden.net

Shorty placket (page 85). Sleeve cuffs (page 93). Hem bands (page 100) with side slits (page 99). **TUNIC FABRIC:** Flannel. **CONTRASTING FABRIC:** Chambray. **LENGTH:** Tunic.

A

B

A. Andrea Verbanic,
evolutionofasewinggoddess.blogspot.com

Bib placket, pleated (page 86). Sleeve cuff (page 93). Hem bands (page 100). **TUNIC FABRIC:** Silk/wool blend. **BIB FABRIC:** Rayon. **LENGTH:** Shortened tunic. **ADDITIONS:** Sleeve plackets.

B. Manju Nittala,
sewmanju.wordpress.com

Outside-facing wide split placket (page 70). Angled collar (page 72). Sleeve cuffs (page 93). **TUNIC FABRIC:** Babycord corduroy. **CONTRASTING FABRIC:** Corduroy. **LENGTH:** Dress. **ADDITIONS:** Back darts.

Marcy Harriell,
oonaballoona.com

Outside-facing wide split placket
(page 70). Angled collar (page 72).
Side slits (page 99). Side zipper
(page 107).
TUNIC FABRIC: Woven blend
LENGTH: Dress
ADDITIONS: Front darts

A

B

C

A. Sallie Barbee, sallieoh.blogspot.com

Scoop neckline with bias band (page 84). Ruffle cuff (page 91).
TUNIC FABRIC: Cotton piqué. **LENGTH:** Dress, hemmed to mini.

B. Sonja Gingerich, gingermakes.com

Outside-facing elongated placket, no contrast (page 75). Sleeveless
armscye finish (page 97). **TUNIC FABRIC:** Linen. **LENGTH:** Dress.

C. Beth Huntington, The Renegade Seamstress, chicenvelopements.wordpress.com

Refashioned dress and skirt. **TUNIC FABRIC:** Cotton.
TRIM: Refashioned belt. **LENGTH:** Tunic.

PATTERN AND FABRIC REQUIREMENTS

The Centerline

The secret to successfully achieving many looks from one pattern is to carefully mark the *centerline* of the neckline plackets or facings and mark the garment from neckline to lengthen/shorten line. It's imperative to always mark the centerline!

We prefer thread tracing, which ensures the centerline is marked on both sides of the garment pieces. Clip a tiny notch on the fold of the front bodice before removing your pattern piece. If your garment is compatible with heat- and water-soluble markers, we recommend that you mark the centerline first, followed by thread tracing. For delicate fabrics, thread trace only.

The Pattern

We suggest that you trace the jumbo tear-out pattern from *The Tunic Bible* onto pattern tracing paper. Tracing the pattern will preserve your original pattern pieces for future use, such as sewing additional variations and sizes.

PATTERN KEYS

Symbol	Meaning
O	Side slit dot
I	Matching points
Arrow	Grain placement

All seam allowances are ⅝″ (1.6 cm) unless otherwise noted.

Fabric Requirements

Yardage quantities noted below are based on making a tunic with the inside-facing V-neck placket (page 78), including sleeves, and in tunic length, unless otherwise noted.

BODICE AND SLEEVE FABRIC REQUIREMENTS

	XS	S	M	L	XL	XXL
45″ wide	2½ yd.	2½ yd.	2⅝ yd.	2⅝ yd.	2⅝ yd.	2¾ yd.
60″ wide	1⅝ yd.	1⅝ yd.	1¾ yd.	1¾ yd.	1¾ yd.	1¾ yd.
115 cm wide	2.30 m	2.30 m	2.40 m	2.40 m	2.40 m	2.60 m
150 cm wide	1.50 m	1.50 m	1.60 m	1.60 m	1.60 m	1.60 m

Fabric Requirements for Optional Elements

Contrasting lower bands and cuffs—add ½ yard / 0.5 m

Contrasting plackets—add ½ yard / 0.5 m

Ruffle neckline—add ½ yard / 0.5 m (Ruffle will be cut on the cross grain.)

Ruffle cuff—add ⅝ yard / 0.6 m for sizes XS, S, and M; add ¾ yard / 0.7 m for L, XL, and XXL

Dress length—add ⅓ yard / 0.3 m

Maxi length—add ¾ yard / 0.7 m

Fusible Interfacing

All sizes—½ yard / 0.5 m

Choosing a Size

The following charts indicate body measurements and finished garment measurements. If your measurements fall between sizes, choose the size closest to your bust measurement.

BODY MEASUREMENTS

		XS	S	M	L	XL	XXL
Bust	in.	33	35	37½	40½	44½	47½
	cm	84	89	95	103	113	121
Waist	in.	28	30	33	36	40	43
	cm	71	76	84	91	102	109
Hips	in.	35½	37½	40	43	47	49½
	cm	90	95	102	109	119	126

FINISHED MEASUREMENTS

		XS	S	M	L	XL	XXL
Bust	in.	35¾	38	40½	43½	47½	50½
	cm	91	97	103	110	121	128
Bust with dart	in.	34½	36¾	39	42	46	49
	cm	88	93	99	107	117	124
Waist	in.	33¾	35½	38	41	45	48
	cm	86	90	97	104	114	122
Waist with dart	in.	30½	32½	35	38	42	45
	cm	77	83	89	97	107	114
Hip	in.	40¾	42¾	45	48½	52½	55½
	cm	104	109	114	123	133	141

Pattern Piece List

Bodice Front	Wide Split Placket	Shorty Placket
Bodice Back	V-neck Placket	Back Neck Facing for V-neck Placket
Sleeve	Elongated Placket	Angled Collar for Wide Split Placket
Bib Placket	Band Collar	Ruffle Cuff Lining

SUPPLIES, NOTIONS, AND ACCESSORIES

Pattern Tracing Paper

- Pellon 830 Easy Pattern

- Pellon 810 Tru-Grid one-inch sheer white polyester craft graph

- Swedish Tracing Paper

Marking Tools

- Pilot FriXion pens: Are you familiar with these heat- and steam-soluble pens? The erasable gel ink comes in assorted colors.

- Water-soluble pens and chalk markers

- Tracing wheel

- Dressmaker's tracing paper: Try the large waxed sheets from Richard the Thread. Yellow and white are our favorite colors.

Adhesives for Attaching Trims

- Dritz Washaway Wonder Tape

- Lite Steam-a-Seam 2

- Fabric glue stick

Measuring Tools

- Seam gauge

- Tape measure

- Large clear quilting ruler

- Large gridded cutting mat

- Clover Press Perfect Hot Hemmer— excellent for making bias tape

- French curve ruler—use for shaping cuffs and hem bands

- 2˝ (5.1 cm) acrylic measuring square for mitered turns

Sewing Accessories

- Glass-head pins

- Scissors

- Hand-sewing needles

- All-purpose thread

- Silk thread for basting

- Top-stitch thread

- Rotary cutter

- Small scissors

- Seam ripper

- Tweezers for removing basting threads

- Point turner

Pressing Tools

- Steam iron

- Tailor's ham

- Clapper/hammer: A hammer? Yes! When heavy seams converge, the gentle tap of a hammer over a press cloth will flatten bulky seams in no time.

- Sleeve board

- Silk organza pressing cloth: A scrap of organza (silk only!) prevents scorching while providing transparency.

- Clover Press Perfect Iron Finger: Use this handy device to save your fingers when you press bias tape.

Interfacing

We prefer a lightweight knit interfacing. Try Pellon EK130 Easy-Knit, a fusible knit interfacing and supple stabilizer for light- to midweight knits and wovens.

SEWING TECHNIQUES

Basic Techniques

Edge stitching: A ⅛″ (0.3 cm) or narrower row of stitching on the edge of the garment that is used wherever close top stitching is required, such as on collars and sleeve cuffs.

Marking the centerline: Mark the center of your Bodice Front with a disappearing marker or thread tracing. This techniques permits perfect placket alignment.

Narrow machine hemming: To achieve a narrow hem finish, mark the desired hemline; then fold the hem ¼″ (0.64 cm) lower than the marked line. Press the fold. Stitch close to the pressed edge and trim any excess fabric close to the stitching line. Fold it again and sew along the hem's top edge.

Stay stitching: Sewing a line of stitching inside the seam allowance right after cutting prevents necklines and armscyes from stretching during construction.

Slip stitching: Use slip stitching to invisibly sew a folded edge into place. It is especially useful for securing sleeve cuffs and neck edge facings inside a collar.

Tacking: Small hand stitches are useful to attach inside-facing plackets and collars to shoulders.

Thread tracing: Outline the centerline, stitching lines, and other pattern markings using long, straight hand stitches in contrasting thread.

Top stitching: A visible stitch used for decorating and finishing garments. Choose a differing color thread for contrast or a thread that matches your fabric.

Underlining: Used to stabilize fabrics and reduce transparency and wrinkles, underlining is cut from the identical pattern pieces and basted to the fashion fabric. The two pieces are treated as one throughout garment construction. Suggested fabrics for underlining include light- to medium-weight cottons and silk organza.

Understitching: This machine stitch, used on the inside edge of necklines and plackets, prevents facings from rolling to the outside by stitching the facing to the seam allowance.

Zipper application: A zipper can be applied to fitted garments. See Side Seam Invisible Zipper Insertion (page 107) for sewing instructions.

Seam Finishes

French Seams

French seams provide a tidy, professional result. Stitch the garment, *wrong* sides together, with ¼″ (0.64 cm) seams. Trim the fabric close to the seam, and press the seam to one side. Turn the garment so the right sides are facing, fold on the seam, and stitch together using a ¼″ (0.64 cm) seam.

Serged Seams

A serger or overlock machine can prevent unraveling by wrapping your fabric edge with looping threads.

Pinked or Zigzagged Seams

Seam finishes needn't be complicated. Trimming seam allowances with pinking shears or sewing a line of zigzag stitching is sufficient to prevent unraveling.

FITTING YOUR MUSLIN

A Well-Fitting Muslin

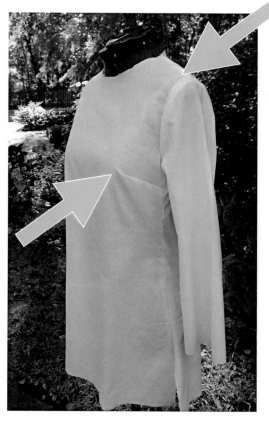

We consider perfecting the bodice muslin (also referred to as *toile*) a must before proceeding with the pattern! The bodice is a simple design, but simplicity requires precision for success.

One of our chief motivations behind writing *The Tunic Bible* was to create a shapely bodice that allows for ease of movement without a sack-like fit. The importance of perfecting the fit of the bodice muslin before cutting into your expensive fashion fabric cannot be overstated, and it is central to the enjoyment and success of sewing our tunics.

Your tunic should be customized to your needs. First, determine the style you desire. Leggings require longer tunic lengths than jeans or pants, for instance. What is your choice of sleeve length? Do you prefer a fitted or relaxed bodice silhouette?

This fitting process takes some time, but once a good fit is achieved, all of the variations are easily attainable.

Bodice Construction

1. Begin your test run by tracing and cutting out the key pattern pieces: *The Tunic Bible* Bodice Front, Bodice Back, and Sleeves (if using).

Note: The term "muslin" comes from the fabric most often used to make a trial sample of a pattern, but you may use a different fabric that is closer in weight and drape to your fashion fabric so that they behave similarly.

2. Using a tracing wheel and dressmaker's tracing paper, transfer all markings and grainlines onto the muslin pieces.

3. Press your muslin. (If you don't press at this point, you won't accurately see the way it will look on your body.)

4. Stitch the pieces together using a long stitch length, which makes for easy disassembly after you have made necessary adjustments to the fit.

5. Check the fit:

- Shoulder seams should be sitting on top of the shoulders.

- Bust darts should be pointing to the apex.

- The waistline marking should hit at the smallest part of the waist.

- The bodice should be flat across the bust without any horizontal pulls (too tight) or gaping (too big).

- Adjust side slits as needed depending upon hem length.

- Customize the hem of the sleeve according to your preference.

Tip

Front and back photographs of yourself in your muslin are great for picking up on issues your eyes can miss when simply viewing in the mirror.

6. Record on your paper pattern (or trace from the fitted muslin) any changes you have made. Identify each muslin piece with the pattern name, date, pattern size, and your current weight.

You now have a perfectly fitted and proportioned tunic bodice—a valuable time saver for the many versions of the tunic you'll want to sew!

Common Adjustments

For details on how to make these adjustments, please refer to your favorite alterations manual. For a list of our suggested alteration guidebooks and online tutorials, see Resources (page 108).

- Full bust adjustment

- Moving bust darts

- Bodice length

- Swayback adjustment

- Hem length and slide slits

GENERAL ASSEMBLY ORDER

Tunic assembly order depends on the neckline, placket, and collar selections.

Wide Split Placket, Bib Placket, Shorty Placket, and Elongated Placket

1 Placket

2 Bust darts

3 Shoulder seams

4 Neckline and collar

5 Side seams

6 Sleeve construction

7 Sleeve insertion

8 Hem

Ruffle Neckline, Inside-Facing V-neck Placket, Outside-Facing V-neck Placket, and Scoop Neckline

1 Shoulder seams

2 Neckline and collar

3 Bust darts

4 Side seams

5 Sleeve construction

6 Sleeve insertion

7 Hem

Seam Finishing Order

All seam allowances are ⅝″ (1.6 cm), unless otherwise noted.

Take pride in your work by ensuring the inside of your tunic looks as good as the outside!

Diligently finishing your seam allowances exhibits evidence of effort and provides professional results. (Refer to Seam Finishes, page 44, as needed.)

Finish the following seam allowances immediately after joining the seams:

• Shoulder seams after joining the front and back bodice sections

• Armscye seams after attaching the sleeve

Finish the following seam allowances prior to joining the seams because they are pressed open:

• Side seam allowances

• Underarm seam allowances

Outside-facing V-neck placket (page 80). Contrasting sleeve cuffs (page 93). Hem bands (page 100). **TUNIC FABRIC:** Refashioned cotton voile scarf. **LENGTH:** Tunic.

A. Inside-facing wide split placket (page 68). Angled collar (page 72).
TUNIC FABRIC: Cotton fabric. **TRIM:** Petersham ribbon. **LENGTH:** Tunic.

B. Shorty placket (page 85). Split cuffs (page 89).
TUNIC FABRIC: Linen. **TRIM:** Purchased appliqué. **LENGTH:** Dress.

C. Outside-facing elongated placket (page 75). Bias neckline finish (page 87). Sleeveless armscye finish (page 97). **TUNIC FABRIC:** Silk dupioni. **TRIM:** Self bias. **LENGTH:** Dress.

Bib placket (page 86). Bias neckline finish (page 87). Contrasting hem bands (page 100).
TUNIC FABRIC: Cotton lawn
LENGTH: Tunic

A. Outside-facing V-neck placket (page 80). Contrasting cuffs (page 93). **TUNIC FABRIC:** Cotton. **TRIM:** Rickrack (page 31). **LENGTH:** Tunic.

B. Inside-facing wide split placket (page 68). Angled collar (page 72). Sleeveless armscye finish (page 97). **TUNIC FABRIC:** Cotton voile. **UNDERLINING FABRIC:** Kona cotton. **TRIM:** Eyelet layered over twill tape (page 102). **LENGTH:** Dress. **ADDITIONS:** Back darts (page 19).

C. Inside-facing wide split placket (page 68). Angled collar (page 72). Sleeveless armscye finish (page 97). **TUNIC FABRIC:** Linen. **TRIM:** Crochet. **LENGTH:** Dress.

D. Inside-facing elongated placket (page 73). Ruffle collar (page 77). Sleeveless armscye finish (page 97). **TUNIC FABRIC:** Silk twill. **LENGTH:** Tunic.

Outside-facing elongated placket (page 75).
Modified band collar (page 76).
BODICE AND SLEEVE FABRIC: Cotton voile
**PLACKET, COLLAR, CUFF, AND
LOWER BAND FABRIC:** Linen
LENGTH: Tunic
ADDITIONS: Invisible side zipper (page 107)

Inside-facing wide split
placket (page 68).
Angled collar (page 72).
TUNIC FABRIC: Linen
TRIM: Petersham ribbon
(page 30)
LENGTH: Tunic

Outside-facing elongated placket (page 75).
Modified band collar (page 76).
Sleeveless armscye finish (page 97).
TUNIC FABRIC: Cotton lawn
TRIM: Self bias trim (page 106)
LENGTH: Tunic
ADDITIONS: Back darts (page 19),
invisible side zipper (page 107)

Inside-facing V-neck placket (page 78).
TUNIC FABRIC: Embroidered
cotton voile fabric
TRIM: Pom-poms (page 31)
LENGTH: Short dress length

A

B

C

D

THE TUNIC BIBLE

E

A. Outside-facing wide split placket (page 70). Angled collar (page 72). Contrasting cuffs (page 93). Contrasting hem bands (page 100). **TUNIC FABRIC:** Linen **LENGTH:** Tunic

B. Inside-facing V-neck placket (page 78). **TUNIC FABRIC:** Recycled cotton sarong. **LENGTH:** Tunic.

C. Inside-facing V-neck placket (page 78). **TUNIC FABRIC:** Cotton ikat. **LENGTH:** Tunic.

D. Ruffle neckline (page 82). Sleeveless armscye finish (page 97). **TUNIC FABRIC:** Cotton twill **LENGTH:** Dress **ADDITIONS:** Back darts (page 19), invisible side zipper (page 107)

E. Inside-facing wide split placket (page 68). Angled collar (page 72). **TUNIC FABRIC:** Linen. **TRIM:** Nylon. **LENGTH:** Tunic. **ADDITIONS:** Back darts (page 19).

A. Inside-facing V-neck placket (page 78). Split sleeve (page 95).
TUNIC FABRIC: Silk/cotton voile. **BODICE UNDERLINING FABRIC:**
Self fabric. **LENGTH:** Tunic.

B. Scoop neckline (page 84). Ruffle cuff (page 91).
TUNIC FABRIC: Four-way stretch cotton jersey . **LENGTH:** Dress.

C. Outside-facing elongated placket (page 75). Band collar
(page 76). Sleeveless armscye finish (page 97).
TUNIC FABRIC: Border-print knit. **TRIM:** Layered ribbon and
metallic. **LENGTH:** Maxi. **ADDITIONS:** Back darts (page 19).

D. Ruffle neckline (page 82). Sleeveless armscye finish (page 97).
TUNIC FABRIC: Silk twill. **LENGTH:** Tunic.

E. Outside-facing wide split placket (page 70). Angled collar
(page 72). Sleeveless armscye finish (page 97).
TUNIC FABRIC: Cotton poplin with Lycra.
TRIM: Embellished ribbon. **LENGTH:** Tunic.
ADDITIONS: Back darts (page 19).

C

D

E

A. Inside-facing wide split placket (page 68). Angled collar (page 72). Sleeveless armscye finish (page 97). **TUNIC FABRIC:** Linen. **TRIM:** Petersham ribbon. **LENGTH:** Dress. **ADDITIONS:** Back darts (page 19), invisible side zipper (page 107).

B. Inside-facing wide split placket (page 68). Angled collar (page 72). **TUNIC FABRIC:** French terry. **TRIM:** Twill tape (page 102). **LENGTH:** Tunic. **ADDITIONS:** Back darts (page 19).

C. Scoop neckline (page 84). Slim sleeves. **TUNIC FABRIC:** Linen jersey. **LENGTH:** Tunic.

D. Ruffle neckline (page 82). **TUNIC FABRIC:** Silk crepe de chine. **LENGTH:** Tunic.

A

B   **C**   **D**

Inside-facing elongated placket (page 73). Bias neckline finish (page 87).
TUNIC FABRIC: Linen
TRIM: Jacquard ribbon (page 102)
LENGTH: Tunic
ADDITIONS: Back darts (page 19)

A. Inside-facing V-neck placket (page 78). **TUNIC FABRIC:** Cotton voile. **TRIM:** Mini pom-poms (page 31). **LENGTH:** Tunic.

B. Round neckline. Fold-over elastic neckline finish. **TUNIC FABRIC:** Silk crochet knit. **LENGTH:** Tunic.

C. Inside-facing wide split placket (page 68). Angled collar (page 72). **TUNIC FABRIC:** Cotton **TRIM:** Twill tape (page 102) **LENGTH:** Tunic **ADDITIONS:** Back darts (page 19)

D. Shorty placket (page 85). Band collar (page 76). Contrasting cuff (page 93). **TUNIC FABRIC:** Cotton gauze. **LENGTH:** Tunic.

E. Outside-facing elongated placket (page 75). Modified band collar (page 76). **TUNIC FABRIC:** Cotton voile. **TRIM:** Self bias (page 106). **LENGTH:** Tunic.

A

A

B

C

A. Inside-facing elongated placket (page 73). Bias neckline finish (page 87). Sleeveless armscye finish (page 97).
TUNIC FABRIC: Cotton. **LENGTH:** Maxi.

B. Inside-facing V-neck placket (page 78). Split sleeve (page 95).
TUNIC FABRIC: Stretch crepe. **LENGTH:** Dress.
ADDITIONS: Back darts (page 19).

C. Inside-facing V-neck placket (page 78). Split cuff (page 89).
TUNIC FABRIC: Viscose jersey. **LENGTH:** Dress.
ADDITIONS: Back darts (page 19).

D. Inside-facing V-neck placket (page 78). Split sleeve (page 95).
TUNIC FABRIC: Silk twill. **LENGTH:** Tunic.

E. Inside-facing wide split placket (page 68). Angled collar (page 72). **TUNIC FABRIC:** Cotton blend knit.
TRIM: Twill tape (page 102). **LENGTH:** Dress.

D

E

A

B

C

A. Scoop neckline (page 84). Knit band neckline (page 84). Slim sleeve. **TUNIC FABRIC:** Knit blend. **LENGTH:** Dress.

B. Ruffle neckline (page 82). Slim sleeve. **TUNIC FABRIC:** Cotton/rayon brocade. **LENGTH:** Dress. **ADDITIONS:** Back darts (page 19), front vertical darts, invisible side zipper (page 107).

C. Inside-facing wide split placket (page 68). Angled collar (page 72). Split cuff (page 89). **TUNIC FABRIC:** Cotton voile. **TRIM:** Petersham ribbon (page 102). **LENGTH:** Tunic.

D. Outside-facing elongated placket (page 75). Band collar (page 76). **TUNIC FABRIC:** Cotton. **LENGTH:** Tunic. **ADDITIONS:** Back darts (page 19).

E. Inside-facing elongated placket (page 73). Modified band collar (page 76). **TUNIC FABRIC:** Linen. **TRIM:** Jacquard ribbon (page 102). **LENGTH:** Tunic.

D

E

Plackets
and Collars

CUTTING

See Fabric Requirements (page 41) for yardage information.

Main Fabric

1 Bodice Front

1 Bodice Back

1 Wide Split Placket

2 Angled Collar

Fusible Interfacing

1 Wide Split Placket

1 Angled Collar

Method

Refer to Sewing Techniques (page 44) as needed. Seam allowance is ⅝˝ (1.6 cm) unless otherwise noted.

1. Staystitch Bodice Front and Bodice Back ½˝ (1.3 cm) from neck edges. This prevents neckline from stretching and allows Angled Collar (page 72) to fit it properly.

2. Mark centerline of Bodice Front and bust darts with thread tracing or disappearing marker. Refer to The Centerline (page 41) for instructions.

3. Iron interfacing to wrong side of Wide Split Placket, following manufacturer's directions.

4. Mark centerline of Wide Split Placket with thread tracing or disappearing marker.

5. Mark V stitching line (center split) on interfaced side of Wide Split Placket with thread tracing or disappearing marker.

6. Finish outside edge by pressing under ½˝ (1.3 cm). Stitch outside edge to finish. *fig. A*

Tip

Run basting stitches along fold line to guarantee precision!

7. With right sides together and centerlines matched, pin Wide Split Placket to Bodice Front. Hand or machine baste along centerlines. Secure with additional pins as needed. *fig. B*

8. Stitch V portion of neckline, reinforcing stitching at center front point.

9. Carefully cut along centerline to point. Trim seam allowance, tapering to center point. Understitch as far as possible to prevent rollout. *fig. C*

10. Turn Wide Split Placket to wrong side of Bodice Front and press. Baste together top neckline edges of Wide Split Placket and Bodice Front. *Note:* Placket will be secured to bodice by trim application and collar. *figs. D & E*

11. Sew bust darts.

12. Sew Bodice Front to Bodice Back at shoulder seams. Finish seam allowances.

13. Apply Angled Collar (page 72).

Refer to General Assembly Order (page 47) to construct rest of garment.

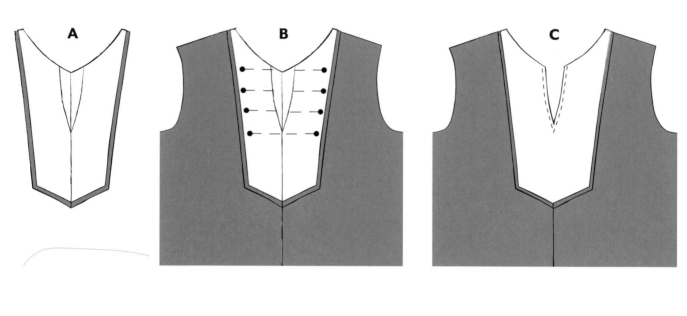

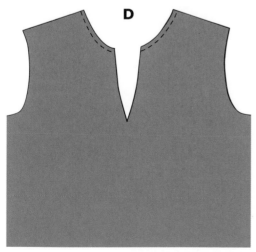

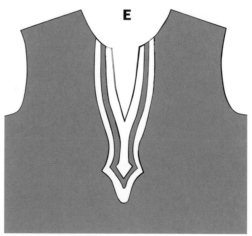

Embellish placket with trim now, if desired.
(See Trimming the Tunic, page 29.)

OUTSIDE-FACING WIDE SPLIT PLACKET
with Angled Collar

CUTTING

See Fabric Requirements (page 41) for yardage information.

Main Fabric

1 Bodice Front

1 Bodice Back

Main or Contrasting Fabric

1 Wide Split Placket

2 Angled Collar

Interfacing

1 Wide Split Placket

1 Angled Collar

Method

Refer to Sewing Techniques (page 44) as needed. Seam allowance is ⅝˝ (1.6 cm) unless otherwise noted.

1. Staystitch Bodice Front and Bodice Back ½˝ (1.3 cm) from neck edges. This prevents neckline from stretching and allows Angled Collar (page 72) to fit it properly.

2. Mark centerline of Bodice Front and bust darts with thread tracing or disappearing marker. Refer to The Centerline (page 41) for instructions.

3. Iron interfacing to wrong side of Wide Split Placket, following manufacturer's directions.

4. Mark centerline of Wide Split Placket with thread tracing or disappearing marker.

5. Mark V stitching line (center split) on interfaced side of Wide Split Placket with thread tracing or disappearing marker.

6. Finish outside edge by pressing under ½˝ (1.3 cm). Do not stitch this edge! *fig. A*

Tip

Run basting stitches along fold line to guarantee precision!

7. Matching centerlines, pin right side of Wide Split Placket to wrong side of Bodice Front. Hand or machine baste along centerlines. Secure with additional pins as needed. *fig. B*

8. Stitch V portion of neckline, reinforcing stitching at center front point.

9. Carefully cut along centerline to point. Trim seam allowance, tapering to center point. Understitch as far as possible to prevent rollout. *fig. C*

10. Turn Wide Split Placket to right side of Bodice Front and press. Baste together top neckline edges of Wide Split Placket and Bodice Front.

11. Pin Wide Split Placket to Bodice Front to secure. Baste outer edge. Topstitch to finish. *fig. D*

12. Sew bust darts.

13. Sew Bodice Front to Bodice Back at shoulder seams. Finish seam allowance.

14. Apply Angled Collar (page 72).

Refer to General Assembly Order (page 47) to construct rest of garment.

A

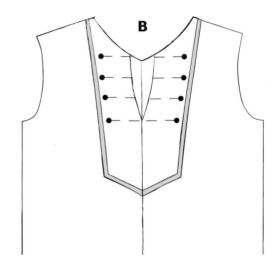

B

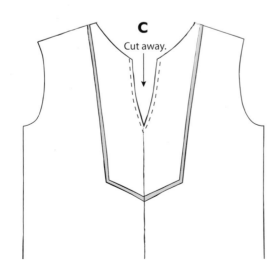

C

Cut away.

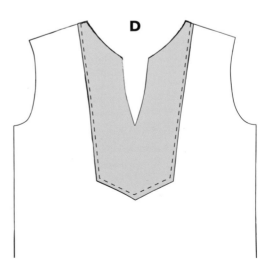

D

Embellish Wide Split Placket or Bodice Front now, if desired. (See Trimming the Tunic, page 29.)

ANGLED COLLAR
for Inside- and Outside-Facing Wide Split Placket

CUTTING

See Fabric Requirements (page 41) for yardage information.

Main or Contrasting Fabric

2 Angled Collar

Fusible Interfacing

1 Angled Collar

Method

Refer to Sewing Techniques (page 44) as needed. Seam allowance is ⅝˝ (1.6 cm) unless otherwise noted.

1. Iron interfacing to 1 Angled Collar piece, following manufacturer's directions. *fig. A*

2. Press under seam allowance on neck edge of Angled Collar without interfacing; trim to ⅜˝ (1.0 cm). *fig. B*

3. With right sides together, pin Angled Collar sections together; stitch top and sides, leaving neck edge open. Trim seam allowances and clip corners. *figs. C & D*

4. Ease stitch neck edges of completed bodice. For proper matching of collar and neckline edges, stitch just below stay stitching. Pin interfaced side of Angled Collar to right side of neckline, matching center backs. Baste and stitch. Trim seam allowance to ⅜˝ (1.0 cm).

5. Pin inside pressed edge of Angled Collar over seam.

6. Using invisible stitches, hand stitch pressed edge of collar along seam (or machine topstitch, if preferred). Press.

Refer to General Assembly Order (page 47) to construct rest of garment.

A

Embellish outer collar (interfaced side) with trim or top stitching now, if desired. (See Trimming the Tunic, page 29.)

B

C

D

Use point turner to turn right side out.

INSIDE-FACING ELONGATED PLACKET
with Bias Neckline Finish

CUTTING

See Fabric Requirements (page 41) for yardage information.

Main Fabric

1 Bodice Front

1 Bodice Back

1 Elongated Placket

1 bias strip 1¾˝ × 18˝ (4.4 cm × 45.7 cm)

Fusible Interfacing

1 Elongated Placket

Method

Refer to Sewing Techniques (page 44) as needed. Seam allowance is ⅝˝ (1.6 cm) unless otherwise noted.

1. Staystitch Bodice Front and Bodice Back ⅜˝ (1.0 cm) from neck edges.

2. Mark centerline of Bodice Front with thread tracing or disappearing marker. Refer to The Centerline (page 41) for instructions.

3. Iron interfacing to wrong side of Elongated Placket, following manufacturer's directions.

4. Mark centerline of Elongated Placket with thread tracing or disappearing marker.

5. Mark V stitching line (center split) of Elongated Placket with thread tracing or disappearing marker.

6. Finish outside edge by pressing under ½˝ (1.3 cm). Stitch outside edge to finish.

Tip

Run basting stitches along fold line to guarantee precision!

7. With right sides together and centerlines matched, pin Elongated Placket to Bodice Front. Secure with additional pins as needed. Hand or machine baste along centerline.

8. Stitch V portion of neckline, reinforcing stitching at center front point.

9. Carefully cut along centerline to point; then trim seam allowance, tapering to center point. Understitch as far as possible to prevent rollout.

10. With Elongated Placket still outside, baste together top neckline edges of Elongated Placket and Bodice Front.

11. Sew Bodice Front to Bodice Back at shoulder seams. Finish seam allowances.

Note: *To finish your tunic with a band collar instead of a bias strip, omit Steps 12–17 and follow the band collar tutorial (page 76).*

---

12. Fold bias strip in half lengthwise, wrong sides together, and press. Mark center back.

13. Pin bias strip to right side of Bodice Front and Bodice Back neck edges, matching center backs and overlapping edges of Elongated Placket by about 1˝ (2.5 cm). Trim excess.

Tip

For smooth bias edging with no puckers, leave a slight bit of ease when pinning bias strip in place.

14. Stitch neck edge using ⅜˝ (1.0 cm) seam allowance.

15. Turn Elongated Placket to inside and press. Use point turner for sharp corners.

16. On wrong side, baste Elongated Placket in place, close to outer edges.

17. On right side, topstitch bias strip ⅜˝ (1.0 cm) from neck edge. Follow basting stitches to topstitch Elongated Placket.

Refer to General Assembly Order (page 47) to construct rest of garment.

OUTSIDE-FACING ELONGATED PLACKET
with Self Bias Trim

CUTTING

See Fabric Requirements (page 41) for yardage information.

Main Fabric

1 Bodice Front

1 Bodice Back

Main or Contrasting Fabric

1 Elongated Placket

1 bias strip 1¾" (4.4 cm) × length of neckline plus 1" (2.5 cm)

Fusible Interfacing

1 Elongated Placket

Method

Refer to Sewing Techniques (page 44) as needed. Seam allowance is ⅝" (1.6 cm) unless otherwise noted.

1. Staystitch Bodice Front and Bodice Back ½" (1.3 cm) from neck edges.

2. Mark centerline of Bodice Front with thread tracing or disappearing marker. Refer to The Centerline (page 41) for instructions.

3. Iron interfacing to wrong side of Elongated Placket, following manufacturer's directions.

4. Mark centerline of Elongated Placket with thread tracing or disappearing marker.

5. Mark V stitching line (center split) of Elongated Placket with thread tracing or disappearing marker.

6. Finish outside edge by pressing under ½" (1.3 cm). Do not stitch this edge!

7. Matching centerlines, pin right side of Elongated Placket to wrong side of Bodice Front. Hand or machine baste along centerlines. Secure with additional pins as needed.

8. Stitch center split neckline marking, reinforcing at center front point.

9. Carefully cut along centerline to point. Trim seam allowance, tapering to center point.

10. Turn Elongated Placket to right side of Bodice Front and press.

11. Pin Elongated Placket to Bodice Front to secure. Baste outer edge. Topstitch to finish. Press.

12. Baste together top neckline edges of Placket and Bodice Front. Embellish Elongated Placket now, if desired. (See Trimming the Tunic, page 29.)

13. Sew bust darts.

14. Sew Bodice Front to Bodice Back at shoulder seams. Finish seam allowances.

15. To finish neckline with bias band, see Bias Band Neckline Finish (page 87). To finish neckline with band collar, see Band Collar (page 76).

Refer to General Assembly Order (page 47) to construct rest of garment.

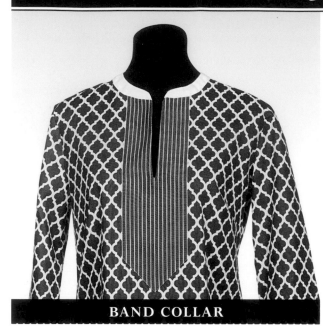

BAND COLLAR

CUTTING

See Fabric Requirements (page 41) for yardage information.

Main or Contrasting Fabric

2 Band Collars

Fusible Interfacing

1 Band Collar

Method

1. Iron interfacing to wrong side of 1 Band Collar, following manufacturer's directions. Mark center back.

2. Press neck edge under ⅜″ (1.0 cm) on Band Collar without interfacing. Trim to ¼″ (0.6 cm). *fig. A*

3. With right sides together, pin Band Collar sections together, leaving neck edge open. Stitch seam. Trim and clip curves. *fig. B*

4. Turn Band Collar and press.

5. Clip Bodice Front and Bodice Back neck edges to stay stitching.

6. Pin interfaced side of Band Collar to right side of neck edge, matching center backs.

7. Baste and stitch using ⅜″ (1.0 cm) seam. Trim seam and clip curves.

8. Press seam toward Band Collar. (A sleeve board is very helpful here.)

9. Pin inside pressed edge of Band Collar over seam. *fig. C*

10. Using invisible stitches, hand stitch along seam (or machine topstitch, if preferred). Press. *fig. D*

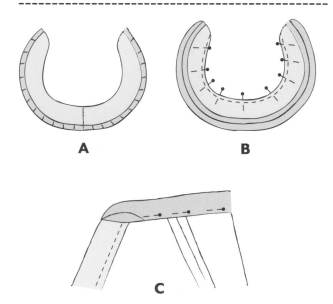

A

B

C

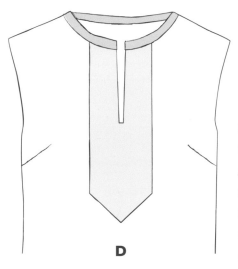

D

Refer to General Assembly Order (page 47) to construct rest of garment.

ONE-INCH RUFFLE

This collar is compatible with the inside-facing elongated placket.

CUTTING

See Fabric Requirements (page 41) for yardage information.

1 piece of fabric cut on cross grain, 3¼˝ (8.3 cm) wide × 2 to 3 times length of neckline*

1 bias band, 1¾˝ wide × 18˝ long (4.4 cm × 45.7 cm) (Or use purchased bias tape.)

*If using lightweight or silky fabric, cut the piece longer. Heavier fabrics require less length.

Method

Refer to Sewing Techniques (page 44) as needed. Seam allowance is ⅝˝ (1.6 cm) unless otherwise noted.

1. Follow Steps 1–9 of Inside-Facing Elongated Placket with Bias Neckline Finish (pages 73 and 74).

2. Sew back to front at shoulder seams. Finish seam allowances.

3. Fold ruffle in half lengthwise, right sides together, and stitch short ends. Clip corners and turn to outside. Press.

4. Baste raw edges together.

5. Gather ruffle to match neckline length.

6. Pin and baste ruffle to outside of neckline.

7. Baste together top neckline edges of Elongated Placket and Bodice Front over ruffle.

8. Fold bias strip in half lengthwise, wrong sides together, and press.

9. Fold strip in half crosswise and mark center.

10. Match center of bias strip to center of back neckline, and pin strip over ruffle along neckline overlapping Elongated Placket by 1˝ (2.5 cm). Trim excess.

Tip

For smooth bias edging with no puckers, leave a slight bit of ease when pinning bias strip in place.

11. Stitch neck edge using ⅜˝ (1.0 cm) seam allowance.

12. Trim stitched edge to ¼˝ (0.64 cm), clipping curves.

13. Turn Elongated Placket and bias band to inside and press. Use point turner for sharp corners.

14. On the inside, slipstitch bias strip in place.

Refer to General Assembly Order (page 47) to construct rest of garment.

CUTTING

See Fabric Requirements (page 41) for yardage information.

Main Fabric

1 Bodice Front

1 Bodice Back

1 V-neck Placket

1 Back Neck Facing

Fusible Interfacing

1 V-neck Placket

1 Back Neck Facing

Method

Refer to Sewing Techniques (page 44) as needed. Seam allowance is ⅝˝ (1.6 cm) unless otherwise noted.

1. Mark centerline of Bodice Front with thread tracing or disappearing marker. Refer to The Centerline (page 41) for instructions.

2. Sew Bodice Front to Bodice Back at shoulder seams. Finish shoulder seam allowances.

3. Iron interfacing to wrong side of V-neck Placket and Back Neck Facing, following manufacturer's directions.

4. Mark centerline on interfaced side of V-neck Placket with thread tracing.

5. With right sides together, sew V-neck Placket to Back Neck Facing at shoulders seams. Press seams open. *fig. A*

6. Finish outside edge by pressing under ⅜˝ (1.0 cm). Stitch outside edge to finish.

7. With right sides together and matching shoulder seams and centerlines, place V-neck Placket over completed bodice neckline. Pin in place. (Excess fabric from Bodice Front and Bodice Back will be trimmed later.) *fig. B*

8. Hand or machine baste upper edge of Back Neck Facing along V-neck Placket seamline. Trim neckline edge of Bodice Front and Bodice Back even with upper edge of V-neck Placket and Back Neck Facing.

9. Stitch seam along basting, pivoting and reinforcing stitching at center front point. *fig. C*

10. Carefully clip to center point; then trim seam allowance to ⅜˝ (1.0 cm), tapering to center point.

11. Clip neck curves and press seam toward V-neck Placket and Back Neck Facing. Turn placket to inside and press.

Refer to General Assembly Order (page 47) to construct rest of garment.

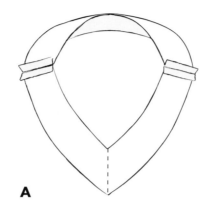

A

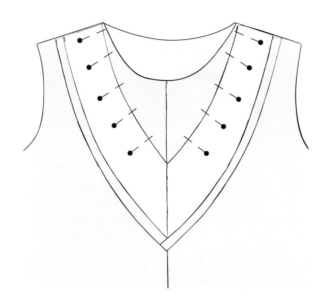

B

C

CUTTING

See Fabric Requirements (page 41) for yardage information.

Main Fabric

1 Bodice Front

1 Bodice Back

Main or Contrasting Fabric

1 V-neck Placket

1 Back Neck Facing

Fusible Interfacing

1 V-neck Placket

1 Back Neck Facing

Method

Refer to Sewing Techniques (page 44) as needed. Seam allowance is ⅝˝ (1.6 cm) unless otherwise noted.

1. Mark centerline of Bodice Front with thread tracing or disappearing marker. Refer to The Centerline (page 41) for instructions.

2. Sew Bodice Front to Bodice Back at shoulder seams. Finish shoulder seam allowances.

3. Iron interfacing to wrong side of V-neck Placket and Back Neck Facing, following manufacturer's directions.

4. Mark centerline on interfaced side of V-neck Placket with thread tracing.

5. With right sides together, sew V-neck Placket to Back Neck Facing at shoulder seams. Press seams open.

6. Press outside edge under ⅜˝ (1.0 cm).

7. With right side of V-neck Placket facing wrong side of completed bodice, place V-neck Placket over bodice neckline, matching at shoulder seams and centerlines. Pin in place. (Excess fabric will be trimmed later.) *fig. A*

8. Hand or machine baste upper edge of Back Neck Facing along V-neck Placket seamline. Trim neckline edge of Bodice Front and Bodice Back even with upper edge of V-neck Placket and Back Neck Facing.

9. Stitch seam along basting, pivoting and reinforcing stitching at center front point. *fig. B*

10. Carefully clip to center point; then trim seam allowance to ⅜˝ (1.0 cm), tapering to center point.

11. Clip neck curves and press seam toward V-neck Placket and Back Neck Facing.

12. Understitch Back Neck Facing seam as far as possible to prevent rollout. Turn piece to outside and press.

13. Baste or pin V-neck Placket in place.

14. Topstitch on outside edge to finish. Press. *fig. C*

Refer to General Assembly Order (page 47) to construct rest of garment.

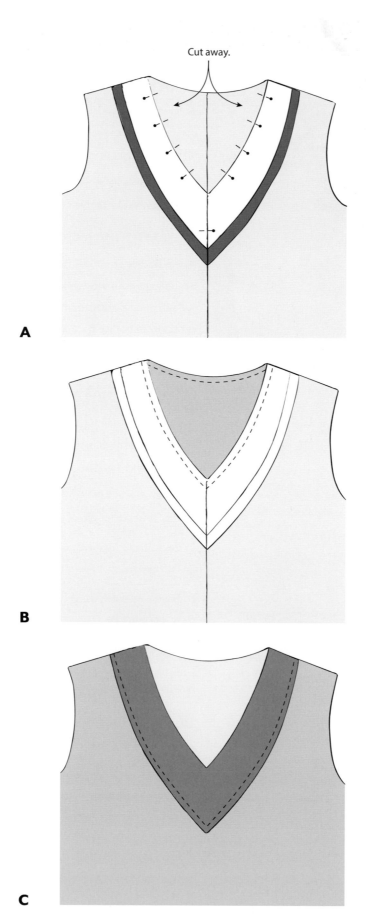

Cut away.

A

B

C

RUFFLE NECKLINE

CUTTING

See Fabric Requirements (page 41) for yardage information.

Main Fabric

1 Bodice Front

1 Bodice Back

1 piece of fabric cut on cross grain, 5˝ (12.7 cm) wide × 2 to 3 times length of neckline* (See Step 5, at right.)

1 seam binding, self made or purchased

*Heavyweight ruffles need less gathering than lightweight. For a stiff ruffle, cut heavyweight fabric twice the length of neckline and lightweight fabric three times the length of neckline.

Method

1. Mark centerline of Bodice front with thread tracing or disappearing marker. Refer to The Centerline (page 41) for instructions.

2. Trace ruffle neck cut line to Bodice Front, and trim. Staystitch ¼˝ (0.6 cm) from neckline, pivoting at corners.

3. Clip each corner diagonally to stitching line. *fig. A*

4. Pin Bodice Front and Bodice Back together at shoulders, beginning from outside shoulder edge. Stitch. Inside edges will not meet due to trimmed front neckline. Trim away excess from Bodice Back at shoulders so that edges are even and back neckline is gently curved. Use French curve ruler (page 43) if necessary. This tool is helpful when drawing soft curves between 2 points.

5. Measure neckline starting at left lower edge of neckline, across back of neck, and around to right lower edge. Record measurement. *fig. B*

6. Fold ruffle in half lengthwise; press and baste raw edges. Gather ruffle to length of neckline plus 1˝ (2.5 cm).

7. Pin ruffle to right side of neckline, extending each end ½˝ (1.3 cm) below lower neckline edges. *fig. C*

8. Baste and stitch using ½˝ (1.3 cm) seam. Trim seam to ⅜˝ (1.0 cm). *fig. D*

9. At lower neckline edge, overlap right ruffle over left and stitch ruffle and lower neckline edges together with ½˝ (1.3 cm) seam. *fig. E*

10. On right side of fabric, topstitch ¼˝ (0.6 cm) from seamline. *fig. F*

Refer to General Assembly Order (page 47) to construct rest of garment.

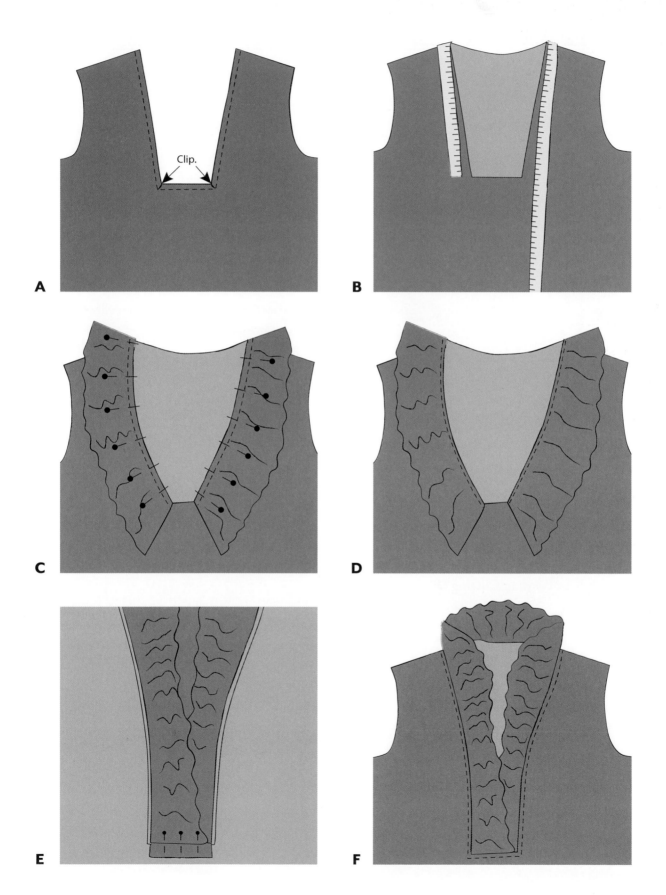

A

Clip.

B

C

D

E

F

SCOOP NECKLINE
with Knit Binding

CUTTING

See Fabric Requirements (page 41) for yardage information.

Main Fabric

1 Bodice Front

1 Bodice Back

1 knit scoop neck binding (Use cutting chart below to find measurement for your size.)

Scoop Neck Knit Binding Cutting Dimensions

Cut 1 from knit fabric.

		XS	S	M	L	XL	XXL
Length	in.	20	20¼	21	21½	22⅜	23
	cm	51	51	53	55	57	58
Width	in.	1¾					
	cm	4.5					

Method

Refer to Sewing Techniques (page 44) as needed. Seam allowance is ⅝″ (1.6 cm) unless otherwise noted.

1. Mark centerline of Bodice Front with thread tracing or disappearing marker. Refer to The Centerline (page 41) for instructions.

2. Staystitch Bodice Front and Bodice Back ¼″ (0.6 cm) from neck edges.

3. Sew bust darts.

4. Sew Bodice Front to Bodice Back at shoulder seams. Finish seam allowances.

5. Sew short ends of band, right sides together. Press seam open.

6. Press knit scoop neck binding in half, wrong sides together. Fold at seam and place pin at opposite fold to mark center front.

7. With right sides together and raw edges aligned, match seam of knit scoop neck binding to Bodice Back neckline center point. Pin center front of knit scoop neck binding to Bodice Front neckline center point. Pin binding evenly to bodice.

8. Starting at center back and sewing with ⅜″ (1.0 cm) seam, attach knit scoop neck binding to completed bodice, stretching binding only until it is slightly taut. Do not stretch bodice! Finish seam allowance with serger, or use another preferred method. Press toward bodice.

9. Using double needle or coverstitch machine, topstitch on right side.

10. Sew Bodice Front and Bodice Back side seams. Finish seam allowances.

Refer to General Assembly Order (page 47) to construct rest of garment.

SHORTY PLACKET
with Bias Neckline Finish

CUTTING

See Fabric Requirements (page 41) for yardage information.

Main Fabric

1 Bodice Front

1 Bodice Back

1 bias strip (See Bias Band Neckline Finish, page 87.)

Main or Contrasting Fabric

1 Shorty Placket

Fusible Interfacing

1 Shorty Placket

- -

Method

Refer to Sewing Techniques (page 44) as needed. Seam allowance is ⅝″ (1.6 cm) unless otherwise noted.

1. Staystitch Bodice Front and Bodice Back ½″ (1.3 cm) from neck edges.

2. Mark centerline of Bodice Front with thread tracing or disappearing marker. Refer to The Centerline (page 41) for instructions.

3. Iron interfacing to wrong side of Shorty Placket, following manufacturer's directions.

4. Mark centerline of Shorty Placket with thread tracing or disappearing marker.

5. Mark V stitching line (center split) of Shorty Placket on interfaced side of Shorty Placket.

6. Finish outside edge by pressing under ½″ (1.3 cm). Do not stitch this edge!

Tip

Run basting stitches along fold line to guarantee precision!

7. Matching centerlines, pin right side of Shorty Placket to wrong side of Bodice Front. Hand or machine baste along centerlines. Secure with additional pins as needed.

8. Stitch V portion of neckline, reinforcing stitching at center front point.

9. Carefully cut along centerline to point. Trim seam allowance, tapering to center point. Understitch as far as possible to prevent rollout.

10. Turn Shorty Placket to outside and press.

11. Pin to secure; then topstitch close to outer edges to finish. Press.

12. Sew bust darts.

13. Sew Bodice Front to Bodice Back at shoulder seams. Finish seam allowances.

14. Finish neckline with Bias Band Neckline Finish (page 87).

Refer to General Assembly Order (page 47) to construct rest of garment.

BIB PLACKET
with Inside Bias Neckline Finish

CUTTING

See Fabric Requirements (page 41) for yardage information.

Main Fabric	Main or Contrasting Fabric	Fusible Interfacing
1 Bodice Front		
1 Bodice Back	1 Bib Placket	1 Bib Placket

Method

Refer to Sewing Techniques (page 44) as needed. Seam allowance is ⅝" (1.6 cm) unless otherwise noted.

1. Staystitch Bodice Front and Bodice Back ½" (1.3 cm) from neck edges.

2. Mark centerline of Bodice Front with thread tracing or disappearing marker. Refer to The Centerline (page 41) for instructions.

3. Iron interfacing to wrong side of Bib Placket, following manufacturer's directions.

4. Mark centerline of Bib Placket with thread tracing or disappearing marker.

5. Mark V stitching line (center split) of Bib Placket with thread tracing or disappearing marker.

6. Press bottom and side edges under ½" (1.3 cm).

7. Matching centerlines, pin right side of Bib Placket to wrong side of Bodice Front. Hand or machine baste along centerlines. Secure with additional pins as needed. *fig. A*

8. Stitch along marked V stitching line, pivoting and reinforcing stitching at center front point.

9. Carefully cut along centerline to point. Trim seam allowance, tapering to center point.

10. Turn Bib Placket to outside and press. *fig. B*

11. Pin to secure; then topstitch close to outer edges to finish. Press.

12. Sew bust darts.

13. Sew Bodice Front to Bodice Back at shoulder seams. Finish seam allowances.

Refer to General Assembly Order (page 47) to construct rest of garment.

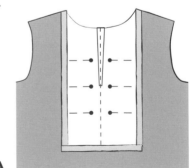

A

B

BIAS BAND NECKLINE FINISH

CUTTING

Main Fabric

1 bias band, 1¾˝ (4.4 cm) wide × length of neckline plus 1˝ (2.5 cm) (Or use purchased bias tape.)

Method

Refer to Sewing Techniques (page 44) as needed. Seam allowance is ⅝˝ (1.6 cm) unless otherwise noted.

1. Press 1 long edge of bias band under ¼˝ (0.6 cm).

2. Pin unfolded edge of bias band to neckline, right sides together, extending bias band ½˝ (1.3 cm) beyond neckline on each side. Stitch neckline seam. *fig. A*

3. Trim stitched edge to ¼˝ (0.6 cm), clipping curves.

4. Press with seam allowance toward bias band.

5. Fold bias band, right sides together, and pin. *fig. B*

6. Mark seamline to match finished edge of placket. Stitch along marked seamline.

7. Trim seam allowance and turn bias band to inside.

8. Finish band edges. For exposed bias band, topstitch or invisibly hand stitch along edges. For clean, concealed finish, double-fold the band to inside. Hand or machine baste in place, and then topstitch to finish. *fig. C*

Refer to General Assembly Order (page 47) to construct rest of garment.

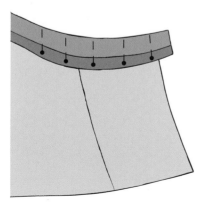

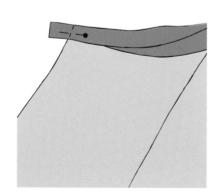

A   **B**   **C**

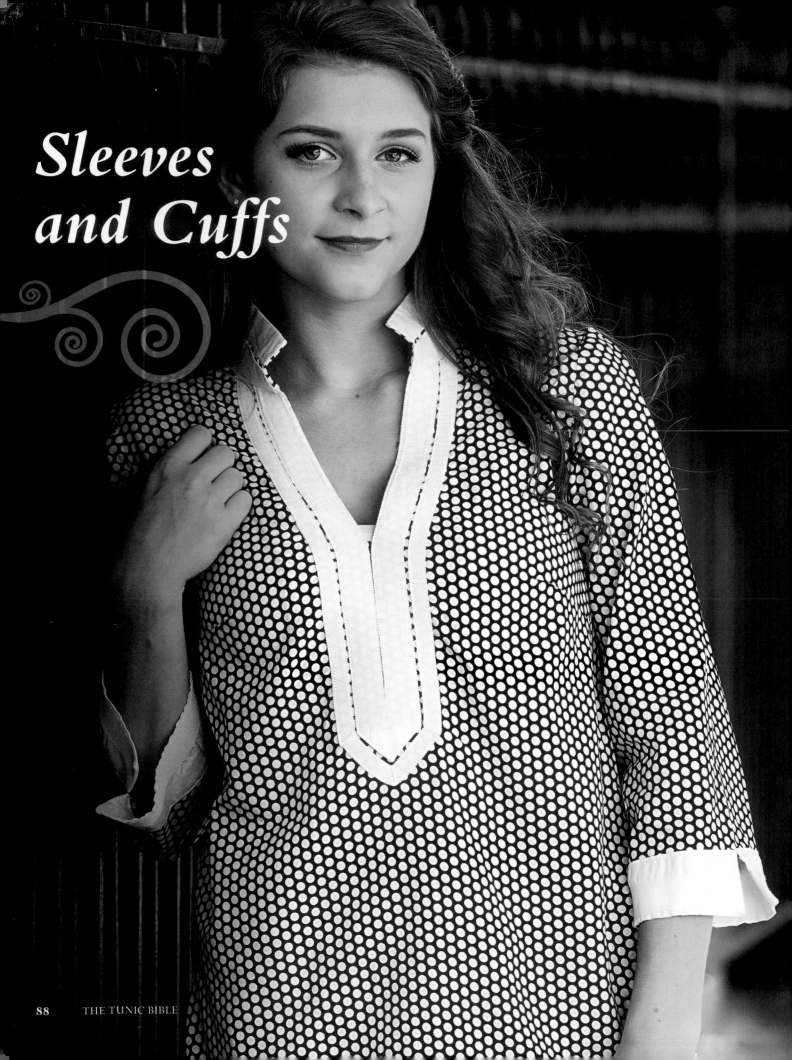

Sleeves and Cuffs

SPLIT CUFF

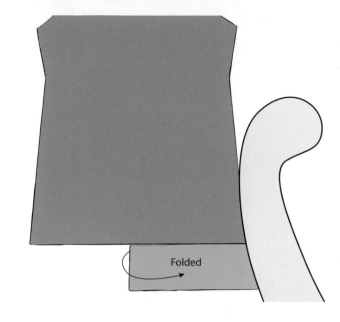

A

Folded

CUTTING

See Fabric Requirements (page 41) for yardage information.

Main Fabric

2 Sleeves

2 pieces of fabric 5˝ (12.7 cm) to 13˝ (33.0 cm) tall × width of Sleeve's lower edge plus 3˝ (7.6 cm)

Mark fold line.

B

Method

Refer to Sewing Techniques (page 44) as needed. Seam allowance is ⅝˝ (1.6 cm) unless otherwise noted.

1. Fold cuff in half lengthwise and then crosswise, so that you will be trimming both ends together.

2. Mark top (raw edge) of cuff to exact width of your Sleeve. Shape cuff, if desired, or cut straight. For flared cuff, use French curve ruler (page 43) to shape cuff. Cut cuff. *fig. A*

3. Open cuff fabric and check measurement. Mark fold line lengthwise down center of fabric. *figs. B & C*

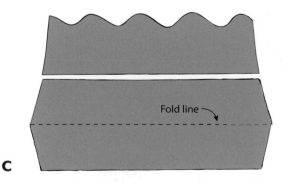

Fold line

C

4. Embellish cuff with trim, if desired. *fig. D*

5. Fold long edge of unembellished side of cuff under ½˝ (1.3 cm). Press. *fig. E*

6. Fold cuff lengthwise on fold line, right sides together, and stitch the ends. Trim seams and turn.

7. Transfer split cuff dot mark from pattern onto Sleeve's center lower edge. Stitch underarm Sleeve seam, right sides together. Finish seam allowances and turn Sleeve, right side facing out.

8. Starting at split cuff dot, pin cuff to Sleeve, right sides together. Cuff ends should meet at split cuff dot. Stitch seam. *fig. F*

9. Clip Sleeve seam allowance to dot. Trim seam allowance and press toward cuff. *fig. G*

10. With invisible stitches, hand stitch pressed edge of cuff to seam allowance. Topstitch if desired.

Refer to General Assembly Order (page 47) to construct rest of garment.

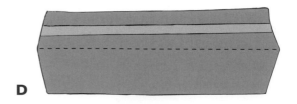

D

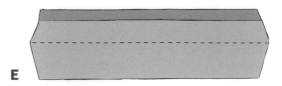

E

F

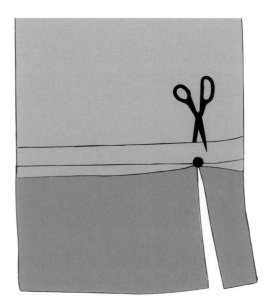

G

RUFFLE CUFF

CUTTING

See Fabric Requirements (page 41) for yardage information.

Main Fabric

2 Sleeves (cut at Ruffle Cuff cut line)

2 Ruffle Cuff Linings

2 ruffles (Use cutting chart below to find measurement for your size and cut on bias.)

Ruffle Cutting Dimensions

Cut 2 on bias.

		XS	S	M	L	XL	XXL
Length	in.	23¼	24¼	25¼	26½	28⅜	29¾
	cm	59	62	64	67	72	76
Width	in.	5½					
	cm	14					

Method

Refer to Sewing Techniques (page 44) as needed. Seam allowance is ⅝″ (1.6 cm) unless otherwise noted.

1. Ease stitch top of Sleeve between matching points.

2. With right sides together, stitch underarm seam. *fig. A*

3. Stitch seam of Ruffle Cuff Linings, right sides together. Fold one edge under ½″ (1.3 cm) and press. *fig. B*

4. Stitch short ends of ruffle with right sides together. Gather both edges of each ruffle. *fig. C*

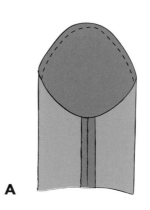

A

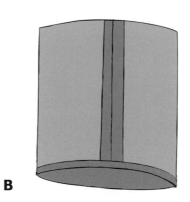

B

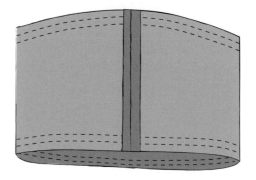

C

5. With right sides together and matching seams, pin ruffle to cuff lining, adjusting gather stitches to fit lining. Hand or machine baste. Stitch, and then open lining so that unstitched edge of lining is free from ruffle. *fig. D*

6. With right sides together and matching seams, pin other gathered edge of ruffle to lower edge of Sleeve. Adjust ruffles. Baste and stitch. Press seam toward ruffle. *fig. E*

7. Turn lining toward wrong side of Sleeve. Pin pressed edge of lining over seam. Slipstitch seam by hand, or baste and topstitch in place. *fig. F*

8. Turn Sleeve, right side facing out. *fig. G*

Refer to General Assembly Order (page 47) to construct rest of garment.

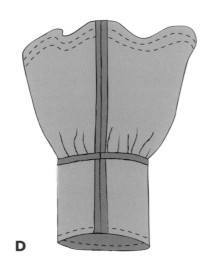

D

E

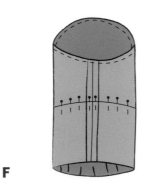

F

G

SLEEVE CUFF

Method

Refer to Sewing Techniques (page 44) as needed. Seam allowance is ⅝˝ (1.6 cm) unless otherwise noted.

1. Place cut fabric, 1 piece at a time, under Sleeve pattern piece. Trim sides even with pattern piece. *fig. A*

2. Fold in half lengthwise and lightly press fold line. Press cuff edge under ½˝ (1.3 cm). If desired, interface cuff from fold line to top of pressed edge, leaving pressed edge free.

CUTTING

See Fabric Requirements (page 41) for yardage information.

Main or Contrasting Fabric

2 pieces 5˝ (12.7 cm) × width of Sleeve's lower edge plus 2˝ (5.1 cm)

Interfacing

2 pieces 2˝ (5.1 cm) × width of cuff

A

3. Fold cuff in half widthwise and sew seam. Stitch underarm seam of Sleeve. *figs. B & C*

4. Slip cuff over lower edge of Sleeve, right sides together, matching seams and raw edges.

5. Sew cuff to lower edge of Sleeve using ½˝ (1.3 cm) seam. Press seam toward cuff and trim. *fig. D*

6. Fold cuff along fold line to wrong side of Sleeve. Pin over seamline. Slipstitch seam by hand, or baste and machine topstitch in place. Press. *fig. E*

Note: *A cuff adds length to a sleeve. Determine length of finished sleeve with cuff before cutting cuff.*

Refer to General Assembly Order (page 47) to construct rest of garment.

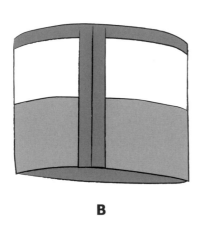

B

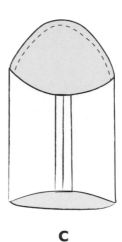

C

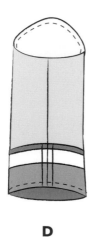

D

E

SPLIT SLEEVE

CUTTING

See Fabric Requirements (page 41) for yardage information.

Main Fabric

2 Sleeves cut in half lengthwise (4 total pieces). See Steps 1–4 (page 96) before cutting.

Method

Refer to Sewing Techniques (page 44) as needed. Seam allowance is ⅝˝ (1.6 cm) unless otherwise noted.

This pattern features three variations of the split sleeve: A, B, and C. *fig. A*

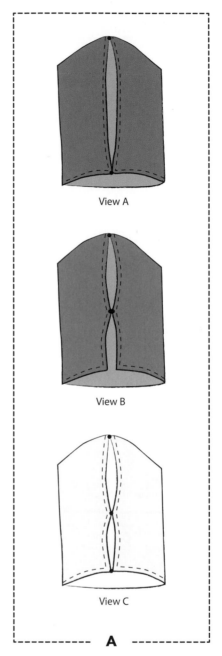

View A

View B

View C

Line drawings—views A, B, and C

1. On Sleeve pattern, extend center grainline from top to bottom of sleeve.

2. Cut along center grainline. *fig. B*

3. Tape 1˝ (2.5 cm) strips of paper to each side of Sleeve along center. *fig. C*

4. Cut 2 pieces of each Sleeve to yield 4 sleeve pieces (2 front and 2 back).

5. Narrowly hem each sleeve piece along center edge. *fig. D*

6. Ease stitch along sleeve cap of all 4 pieces.

7. Place original Sleeve pattern underneath Sleeve pieces. Place top edge of front Sleeve over top edge of back Sleeve, and pin to conform to original Sleeve pattern. Baste overlapping sections together at top edge. *fig. E*

8. Sew underarm seam at seamline, using traditional straight seam or French seam.

9. Views A and C: Pin lower edge of Sleeve together and narrowly hem lower edge of sleeve.

View B: Do not pin lower edge of Sleeve. Narrowly hem bottom edges.

10. Attach Sleeve to bodice. Finish shoulder seam.

11. Views B and C: Try on bodice and mark Sleeve at elbow. Tack Sleeve front to back above elbow.

Refer to General Assembly Order (page 47) to construct rest of garment.

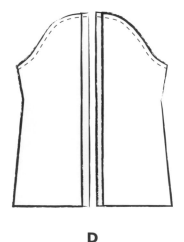

B

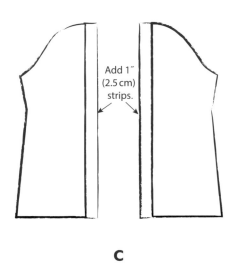

Add 1˝ (2.5 cm) strips.

C

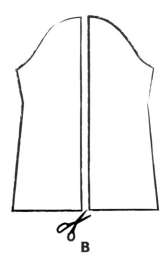

D

E

CUTTING

See Fabric Requirements (page 41) for yardage information.

Main Fabric

Self-made or purchased seam binding

A

Method

Refer to Sewing Techniques (page 44) as needed. Seam allowance is ½" (1.3 cm).

If using purchased seam binding, begin with the instructions in Attaching Seam Binding (below).

Making Seam Binding

1. Cut 2 bias strips 1¾" (4.4 cm) wide × circumference of armscye + 2" (5.1 cm).

2. Fold bias strip in half lengthwise and press. *fig. A*

Attaching Seam Binding

1. Staystitch armscye.

2. Fold end of seam binding in ¼" (0.6 cm).

3. Pin folded end of seam binding at underarm. Pin seam binding around armscye, slightly overlapping end over folded edge at beginning. Baste. *fig. B*

4. Stitch raw edges of bias binding to armscye, using ½" (1.3 cm) seam.

5. Trim seam.

6. Fold binding to inside and stitch pressed fold over seam allowance by hand using invisible stitches (or machine topstitch). Press. *fig. C*

Refer to General Assembly Order (page 47) to construct rest of garment.

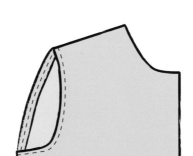

B   **C**

Other Techniques

SIDE SLITS

Method

Refer to Sewing Techniques (page 44) as needed. Seam allowance is ⅝″ (1.6 cm) unless otherwise noted.

1. Finish side edges of Bodice Front and Bodice Back with serger (or other preferred method) from underarm to hem.

2. With right sides together, stitch side seam of Bodice Front and Bodice Back from underarm to side slit dot. Press open entire length of side seam. *fig. A*

3. Double-fold Bodice Front and Bodice Back side seam allowances to inside from side slit dot to hem. Press. *fig. B*

4. Starting at Bodice Front lower hem, topstitch side slit, pivoting at corners and ending at Bodice Back lower hem. Press. *fig. C*

Refer to General Assembly Order (page 47) to construct rest of garment.

A

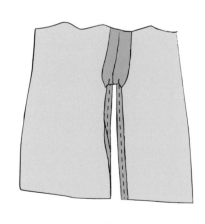

B

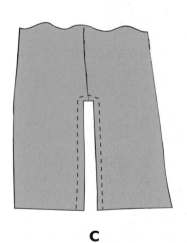

C

CUTTING

Contrasting Fabric

2 pieces 7˝ (17.8 cm) × width of Bodice Front's lower edge plus 2˝ (5.1 cm) (See Step 5, at right.)

Method

Refer to Sewing Techniques (page 44) as needed. Seam allowance is ⅝˝ (1.6 cm) unless otherwise noted.

1. Finish Bodice Front and Bodice Back side seam allowances from underarm to hem, using serger or other method.

2. With right sides together, stitch Bodice Front and Bodice Back side seam from underarm to side slit dot. Press side seam open from underarm to hem.

3. Double-fold the side slit seam allowance to inside, below side vent slit. Press.

4. Starting at lower edge of Bodice Front, baste side slit, pivoting at corners and ending at lower edge of Bodice Back.

5. Cut 2 fabric bands 7˝ (17.8 cm) long × width of Bodice Front's lower edge plus 2˝ (5.1 cm). *fig. A*

6. Press each long edge under ½˝ (1.3 cm). *fig. B*

7. Fold in half lengthwise, right sides together. Place under bodice and trim excess, leaving ⅝˝ (1.6 cm) seam allowance. *fig. C*

8. Pin and stitch short edges. Trim seam allowance and clip corner points. Turn and press. *fig. D*

9. Insert bottom edge of Bodice Front into band, ensuring raw edge meets inside bottom fold of band and corners fit smoothly. *fig. E*

10. Pin in place and topstitch close to upper edge of hem band. *fig. F*

11. Construct and apply back hem band in same manner.

12. Starting at lower edge of front hem band, topstitch side vent, pivoting at corners and ending at lower edge of back hem band. Remove basting. Press. *fig. G*

Refer to General Assembly Order (page 47) to construct rest of garment.

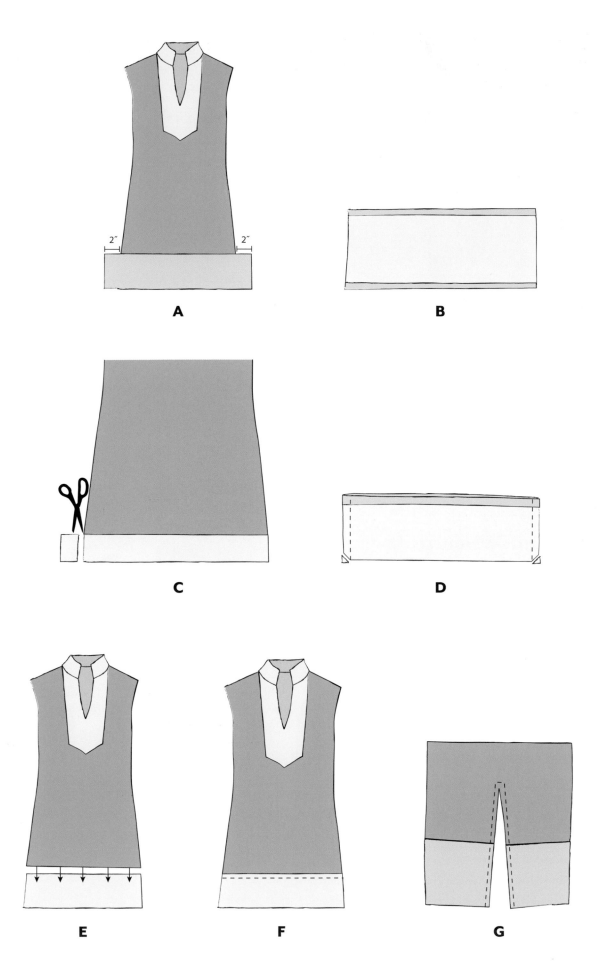

A

B

C

D

E

F

G

How to Apply Trim

Our single favorite notion for applying trim is fabric adhesive tape. Available in both water-soluble and permanent varieties, these products firmly anchor your embellishments without pins, which often cause shifting and distortion.

Using this time-saving notion allows you to lift and rearrange your trim until you are pleased with its placement.

Always prepare your trim by laundering it in the same manner as the fabric to which it will be applied.

Sharp mitered corners and crisp angles are a must when applying trim. Careful symmetry when using patterned trims makes all the difference between a look that is professionally sewn and one that shouts "homemade."

Where and When to Apply Trim

Plackets: Attach the placket to the Bodice Front and apply trim prior to sewing bust darts.

V-neck: Apply trim after sewing shoulder seams and attaching the V-neck Placket and facing.

Collar: Apply trim before sewing two collar sections together.

Sleeves: Apply trim before sewing the underarm Sleeve seam.

Sleeve Band and Cuff: Apply trim to the interfaced side of a cuff or band before enclosing it in a seam.

Lower Edge and Side Slits: Apply trim after hemming the tunic front and back. Lower edges and side slits are double folded and topstitched.

Photo by William Gunn

Mitered Corner Application

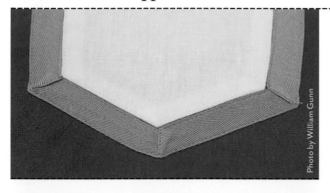

1. Cut length of trim equal to outside edge of placket plus 2˝ (5.1 cm). For hem bands, measure front and back lower edges, including length of side slits plus 4˝ (10.2 cm). Apply adhesive tape to reverse side of trim, following manufacturer's directions, and lightly finger-press into place. To avoid puckers after laundering, do not stretch trim when applying.

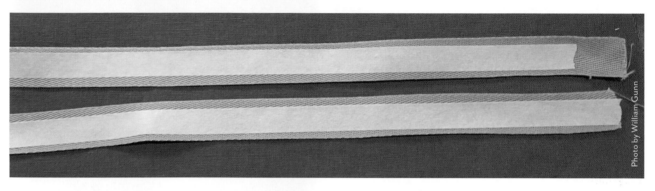

2. For placket, begin at neckline and follow outline of placket's finished edge. Fold trim at 30° or 45° angle at each corner, depending on placket shape. Add pins to secure. Steam iron to shape curved areas as needed.

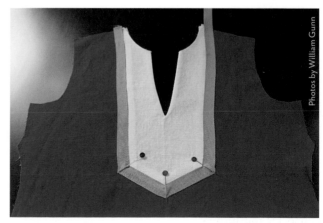

3. Stitch close to inside and outside edges of trim, including folded edges of mitered corners.

For lower edge trim, begin at center back and fold 45° angles at side seam slit to go up side of slit; then form folds at 45° angle inside and outside to continue down other side of side seam slit. Continue along Bodice Front lower edge to opposite side seam, repeating 45° angles.

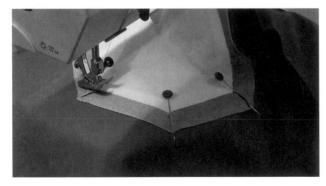

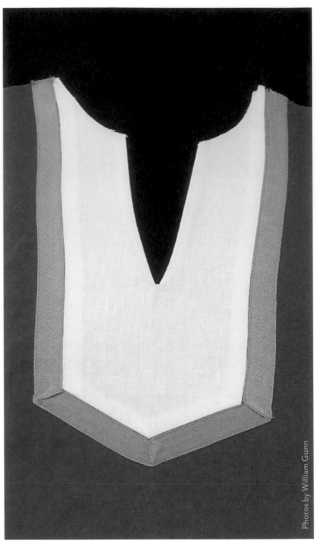

Photos by William Gunn

V-fold Application

1. Follow Steps 1 and 2 of Mitered Corner Application to measure trim and apply adhesive tape.

2. Follow outline of finished placket edge or side slit. Fold trim at 45° angle to form desired width of V. Form second 45° angle, reversing directions.

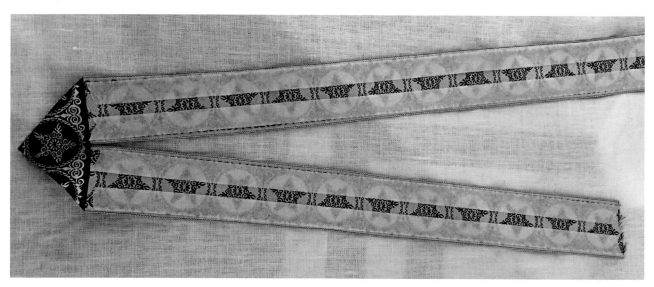

3. Stitch close to inside and outside edges of trim, including folded edges of mitered corners.

CUTTING

½ yard (0.5 m) of fabric will yield 23˝ (50 cm) pieces of 1¾˝ (4.4 cm) bias strips. If you don't want a pieced strip for placket trim, start with ¾ yard (0.7 cm) of fabric.

Method

1. Place fabric on cutting mat and cut in half along 45° angle line.

2. Place cut bias edge of piece on cutting mat along vertical cutting line. Fold in half along vertical line, if needed, to fit piece on cutting mat. Cut 1¾˝ (4.4 cm) bias strips using quilting ruler and rotary cutter. If you have no cutting mat, fold square on diagonal, crease, and cut along crease. Cut strips parallel to this bias cut.

3. Sew strips together to desired length.

    Average length required for:

    Placket trim—35˝ (89 cm) per row

    Collar—16˝ (41 cm) per row

    Sleeve—18˝ (46 cm) per row

    Front and back lower edge only—57˝ (145 cm) per row

    Front and back lower edge and side slits—85˝ (216 cm) per row

4. Fold and press ½˝ (1.3 cm) along long edge to make ¾˝ (1.9 cm)-wide trim using your favorite method. Using your Clover Hot Hemmer as a guide, fold and press one side of strip up ½˝ along hemmer marking.

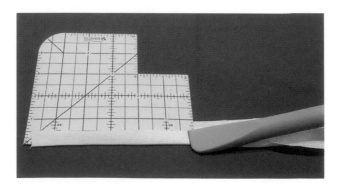

5. Turn fabric so that pressed edge is on top. Place Hot Hemmer on top of strip, with ½˝ marker even with pressed edge. Press up lower edge.

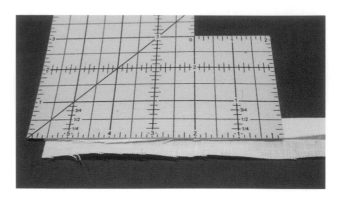

6. Turn and check measurements.

7. Press top of tape to sharpen edges.

Tip

Don't burn your fingers! The Clover Press Perfect Iron Finger is an excellent accessory for making bias tape. (See Supplies, Notions, and Accessories, page 43.)

SIDE SEAM INVISIBLE ZIPPER
Insertion

Follow Assembly Instructions as determined by your neckline design. The zipper is inserted on the left side seam at the time of side seam construction.

Method

1. Cut 2 strips of interfacing ⅝″ (1.6 cm) × length of zipper, and apply to wrong side of side seams. Finish seam allowances. Do not stitch seams! Press ⅝″ (1.6 cm) seam allowance along each side seam.

2. Place zipper on side seam, with top of zipper tape even with top of side seam.

3. Mark placement of zipper stop, and then mark 1½″ (3.8 cm) below zipper stop.

4. Starting at bottom, stitch side seam to lower mark.

5. Open zipper and place face down on right side of fabric with zipper teeth along pressed edge, facing away from fabric edge. *fig. A*

6. Pin in place, and using your invisible zipper foot, stitch until you reach top of zipper stop.

7. Close zipper and mark zipper stop on remaining seam. Open zipper and pin remaining side. Check to make sure top tabs are even. *fig. B*

8. Stitch to top of zipper stop, keeping seamline on left of needle. Close zipper and turn fabric to wrong side. *fig. C*

9. With regular zipper foot, stitch between lower seam and zipper stop. Press seam open.

10. Stitch lower edge of zipper tape to seam allowance to stabilize.

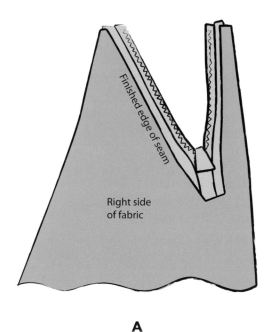

Finished edge of seam

Right side of fabric

A

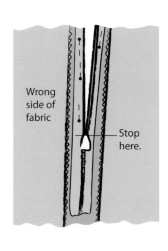

Wrong side of fabric

Stop here.

B

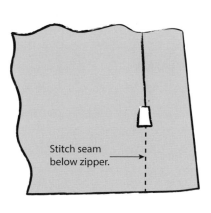

Stitch seam below zipper.

C

RESOURCES

Fabric

In the Garment District of New York City

B&J Fabrics—B&J Fabrics, located on 7th Avenue, may be the most organized fabric store on the planet. Specializing in high-end fabrics, the store features beautiful cottons, laces, silks, faux furs, and specialty fabrics. The online store provides international shipping. • *bandjfabrics.com*

Elliott Berman Textiles—When in New York, be sure to visit Elliott Berman Textiles. The store carries a variety of designer fabrics, and we really love the large collection of French and Italian high-quality viscose. • *elliottbermantextiles.com*

Mood Fabrics—Located in the heart of the garment district, the *Project Runway* go-to store has it all! Serving more than 1,200 customers a day, Mood Fabrics is a destination fabric paradise. The store is recognized for its variety of fabrics, competitive prices, and customer service. If a trip to New York is not possible, visit the comprehensive online store. Mood Fabrics also has a store in Los Angeles, California. • *moodfabrics.com*

Rosen & Chadick Fabrics—Featuring beautiful designer fabrics from all over the world, this lovely store offers high-quality linen in more than 125 colors. It does not currently sell fabric online. • *rosenandchadickfabrics.com*

On the West Coast

Britex Fabrics—A San Francisco landmark since 1952, Britex Fabrics is a must-visit store when on the West Coast. Four floors of fabrics, trim, and sewing tools offer something for everyone. Britex also offers an excellent online store. • *britexfabrics.com*

Michael Levine, Inc.—With a unique selection of hard-to-find fabrics, Michael Levine, Inc. offers a huge, nicely categorized store. The online store's fast shipping is a true bonus. • *lowpricefabric.com*

When in Rome (International Stores)

Linton Tweeds	**Liberty**	**Valli Tessuti Alta Moda**
Carlisle • England	England	Milan, Rome, Florence • Italy
lintondirect.co.uk	*liberty.co.uk*	*vallitessuti.com/?lang=en*
Casa dei Tessuti	**Janssens & Janssens**	**General Diff**
Italy	France	France
casadeitessuti.com	*janssensparis.com*	*generaldiff.com*

On Your Device

Emma One Sock—Two thumbs up for this online store! The customer service is exceptional. Every fabric is beautifully photographed and listed with the Pantone identification number. The suggested coordinating fabrics will lead you to purchases you never imagined! Emma One Sock stocks a large selection of high-quality linen knits. • *emmaonesock.com*

Marcy Tilton—Marcy Tilton brings creative energy to the sewing industry with artful patterns, trips to Paris, and a fantastic online store featuring a fabulous collection of knits and more! • *marcytilton.com*

Gorgeous Fabrics—Fabulous finds are always available at Gorgeous Fabrics, including a large selection of silks, cottons, and knits. We find the product descriptions, which include the Pantone identification numbers, very helpful. *gorgeousfabrics.com*

Hawthorne Threads—A great online supply of the latest cotton collections from Amy Butler, Michael Miller, Riley Blake, Robert Kaufman, and more. We also like the fast delivery service. • *hawthornethreads.com*

Sawyer Brook—Primarily a mail-order service, Sawyer Brook maintains a warehouse open to the public and prides itself on exceptional customer service. That, combined with great tunic fabrics such as silk blends and stretch wovens, makes this online store a winner. *sawyerbrook.com*

NY Fashion Center Fabrics—This online store offers a very large selection of linens and silks. We recommend ordering samples for color and weight! *nyfashioncenterfabrics.com*

Girl Charlee—A great resource for casual tunic fabrics! *girlcharlee.com*

Spoonflower—Design your own fabric at Spoonflower, where the possibilities are indeed endless! Spoonflower offers thousands of designs and nearly twenty fabric choices, including a variety of cotton wovens, knits, and even silk crepe de chine. We recommend ordering a sample of all its unprinted swatches for just a dollar before taking the plunge. Be prepared to spend hours on this compelling site! • *spoonflower.com*

Trim

The Sewing Place offers petersham ribbon in dozens of colors and several sizes. *thesewingplace.com > Search "petersham ribbon"*

M&J Trimming has a spectacular selection of trims at its New York City store. The online store is somewhat limited by comparison. • *mjtrim.com*

Mokuba, New York, located in the heart of the garment district, features 50,000 exquisite ribbons and trims designed and manufactured by Mokuba Co. Ltd. in Japan. *www.mokubany.com*

Etsy features a constantly changing list of online vendors. We recommend visiting Etsy's website and bookmarking a few favorites. We have purchased lovely jacquard, appliqués, and twill tape from Etsy. Several Etsy vendors sell a variety of colorful twill tape widths in wholesale quantities. *etsy.com*

Various websites also carry cotton twill tape by the yard in white, natural, and navy. We suggest conducting an Internet search for these colors of cotton twill tape.

Sewing and Alterations

Books

1,000 Clever Sewing Shortcuts and Tips by Deepika Prakash, 2010, Creative Publishing International.

The Sewtionary by Tasia St. Germaine, 2014, KP Craft.

The Complete Photo Guide to Perfect Fitting by Sarah Veblen, 2012, Creative Publishing International.

Pattern Fitting with Confidence by Nancy Zieman, 2008, KP Craft.

Fitting & Pattern Alteration by Elizabeth Liechty, Della Pottberg-Steineckert, and Judith Rasband, 2009, Fairchild Books.

Online Classes and Links

Sewing Basics by Deepika Prakash
patternreview.com > Online Classes > All Classes > Choose Class > Sewing Basics

Bust Adjustments by Sarah Veblen
patternreview.com > Online Classes > All Classes > Choose Class > Bust Adjustments

Adjust the Bust by Kathleen Cheetham
craftsy.com > Search "Adjust the Bust"

Full Bust Adjustment on a One-Dart Bodice by Mary Danielson Perry of Curvy Sewing Collective
curvysewingcollective.com > Search "Full Bust Adjustment"

Removing Bust Darts from a Pattern by Maria Denmark
mariadenmark.com > Search "Removing Bust Darts"

Moving a Bust Dart by Roseana Auten, Burda Style
burdastyle.com > Search "Moving a Bust Dart" and click the title under "Techniques"

Custom Fitting: Back, Neck, and Shoulders by Kathleen Cheetham
craftsy.com > Search "Custom Fitting Back, Neck, and Shoulders"

Underneath It All: Guide to Interfacings, Linings & Facings by Linda Lee
craftsy.com > Search "Underneath It All"

Sewing with Specialty Fabrics

BOOKS

Sew Knits with Confidence by Nancy Zieman, 2013, Krause Publications.

Linen and Cotton: Classic Sewing Techniques for Great Results by Susan Khalje, 1999, Taunton Press.

ONLINE CLASSES

The Essential Guide to Sewing with Lace by Alison Smith
craftsy.com > Search "Essential Guide to Sewing with Lace"

Sewing with Silks: The Liberty Shirt by Linda Lee
craftsy.com > Search "Sewing with Silks"

ABOUT THE AUTHORS

Sarah Gunn is a resident of Spartanburg, South Carolina. Her commitment to living with creativity and purpose is demonstrated through her life of many roles and responsibilities. Creator of the popular sewing blog *Goodbye Valentino*, Sarah is also a wife, mother, arts advocate, and community leader. She is a former symphony orchestra executive director and mentor of classical musicians. Seeking excellence in all of her endeavors, including the pursuit of a stylish wardrobe without spending an excessive amount of money, she was inspired to renew the sewing skills she developed as a teenager by passionately sewing her own clothes.

One year after creating *Goodbye Valentino*, Sarah became affiliated with Mood Fabrics, the fabric store of television's *Project Runway*, by representing the store's online sewing network.

Featured in *Vogue Patterns* magazine as well as other sewing industry and regional publications, Sarah was voted a Top 50 Blogger for Burda Style in 2014 and 2015. She is also recognized for hosting Ready-to-Wear Fasts, in which readers are encouraged to make their own clothes for one year instead of buying them. She continues to inspire thousands of women to sew clothes.

Julie Starr resides on a barrier island off Charleston, South Carolina. She is a favorite contributor to the website *Sewing Pattern Review*, which has a 300,000+ global membership. On the website, her clothing has won four consecutive annual awards based on member votes, and she was recently profiled as the site's "Member in Focus." Julie has been an active participant in the *Goodbye Valentino* Ready-to-Wear Fasts. Her career in custom luxury homebuilding on Kiawah Island, S.C., provides a skill set that translates easily to garment design and construction. The natural beauty of South Carolina's Lowcountry beaches, tidal marsh, and diverse flora and fauna, along with the history and charm of historic Charleston, provide much of her design inspiration and are reflected in her work. Julie is a Master Gardener, and when not in her sewing room she can be found in her garden, with her husband on the golf course or keeping their wire fox terrier out of mischief.

Want even more creative content?

Make it,
snap it,
share it
using
#ctpublishing